"This book is an intriguii
dynamics of discipleship. I
it, is an intrinsic part of what it means to imitate Christ and
therefore to follow him. By cleverly mixing theology with social
science, Phil helps us understand a basic aspect of relationship
with Jesus."

Alan Hirsch
Founder of Future Travelers / Forge Missional Training
Network. Author, *The Permanent Revolution, Untamed,* and *The
Faith of Leap*

"God-given potential, deep spirituality, mentors who
strategically walk with us—these are the makings of immense
creativity and influence. *Copycat* leads us into this life-consuming
adventure of discovering our originality and living out God's
unique plan for each of our lives. Along the steps of this journey
Phil Zarns guides us in an engaging, personal way, with a style
that is authentically thoughtful and entertainingly creative."

Jim Bradford
General Secretary for The Assemblies of God, USA

"Once in a great while, we discover a book whose author takes
something commonly talked about but little understood and
makes it refreshingly obvious and practical. Phil Zarns has
accomplished just that—and delightfully so—with *Copycat.* The
whole concept of mentoring modeled by Jesus and so crucial to
discipleship has become popular but too infrequently practiced in

daily life. Using scientific concepts (surprise!) and reader-friendly illustrations from everyday life and culture, Zarns unpacks our human propensity for mimicry and integrates it with the spiritual processes of discipleship and becoming more and more like Christ. Engaging, articulate, and biblically grounded, *Copycat* is a gift to those who are serious about mentoring people to follow Jesus in our 21st century world."

Dr. Beth Grant
Project Rescue
Professor, Assemblies of God Theological Seminary
Author, *Courageous Compassion*

"The sense of belonging is one of the deepest needs we have as human beings. As a Christian, I do believe we are created to live in the likeness of our God, a likeness which includes true relations and an ongoing process of maturing in Christ. Phil Zarns is giving us a good help in walking with Jesus in today's culture. Here in Sweden we live with strong secular-rational values and also a strong individualistic self-expressing trend. In that environment we need this book, which I warmly recommend for reading."

Daniel Alm
Lead Pastor, Pingst Västerås, Sweden

"When I was growing up, to be called a 'copycat' was an insult. Phil Zarns will make you think about that name in an entirely different way. From the beginning of life, we mimic what we see and hear. Much of what we do and say is the result of mimicking those we admire. In essence, we are all copycats! The key question is not 'Are you a copycat?' but 'Who are you copying?' *Copycat* is a fresh new take on learning, and the process of making disciples. After reading this book, you'll want to be called a copycat!"

Rod Loy
General Presbyter
Pastor, First Assembly of God, North Little Rock, AR
Author, *Immediate Obedience*

"Phil Zarns writes with the heart of a pastor, the experience of a seasoned leader, and the humor of a late-night talk host. I enjoyed *Copycat* immensely as I laughed through the pages of impactful discipleship principles. Phil has provided a refreshing perspective on mentoring through this book."

Aaron Allison
Lead Pastor, Church at Indian Lake, Nashville, TN

"Impressed with Phil's approach, I appreciate the non-confrontational style and the soft approach to truth—yet it comes across without compromise!"

Greg Mundis
Director of World Missions for The Assemblies of God USA

"In *Copycat*, Phil Zarns inspires to personal development using everyday-life metaphors and points out the role models around us. *Copycat* guides with humor when it comes to growing our relationship with our Creator and Savior. The author is a man of integrity and humility and this book is a reflection of his life. It will help you move from the complex of comparison and release you on the journey called lifelong learning. Phil Zarns combines his creative expressions with a warm and personal tone. Read this!"

Lydia and Nicklas Mörling
Pastors, Twentyfour Church, Stockholm, Sweden

"In a day and age when almost anything can be replicated and copied, this world is desperate for real, authentic, and transparent leadership in churches. If we are going to reach the next generation, we need to be the best versions of who God created us to be. It is time to stop copying what works for other people and start reaching people with the gifts and callings God has given us!"

Rob Ketterling
Lead Pastor, River Valley Church, Apple Valley, MN
Author, *Change Before You Have To, Thrill Sequence*

"Phil Zarns has taken a phrase, 'copycat,' which generally has a negative connotation, and turned it around to capture the heart of discipleship and training. In his ministry setting, he's discovered that if he does not train leaders, his ministry will die when he leaves. This is true for all of us. He's strived to live his life by copying what Jesus did. *Copycat* will inspire each of us to be better mentors and coaches."

Clarence St. John
Superintendent, Minnesota District of the Assemblies of God

"This book shines with Phil's characteristic brilliance and kindness. Phil has the rare ability to clearly see the truth hidden in plain sight all around us. *Copycat* brings us back to an idea that happens to be the foundation Christ built his kingdom on. It unlocks the ways to make a lasting impact that have been lost for ages. If you want to have a big impact in individual lives, *Copycat* shows you how. My recommendation is: do not read this book alone."

Ryan Skoog
Missionary Entrepreneur
Co-Founder of Venture Expeditions, Fly for Good, Volunteer Card, Workshop Chicago, Faith Ventures

"When I was in my twenties, I wanted to play the electric guitar just like Phil Zarns. He could captivate the audience with his skill, style, and all-round finesse. I would stand in the crowd just watching him effortlessly work his craft. Almost twenty years later, I could never imitate his prowess on the guitar, but I sit back and dream of replicating his craftsmanship with words such as I read in *Copycat*.

"Phil in his thought-provoking writing brings me on a journey through history, science, and personal stories. He looks at and studies others, but he ultimately brings me to a place of understanding myself. It is when I start to embrace the idea of mimicking mentors, parents, professionals, and ultimately Jesus, that I start to truly find my voice. I gave up trying to play guitar like Phil, but his writing inspires me to be a better author and communicator.

"After reading *Copycat* you will be inspired to become the individual that Jesus has designed you to be. Go on a journey with Phil Zarns through *Copycat*, and you just might find out that being a copycat will help you be the original you so desire to be."

Joseph Fehlen
Author, *Ride On*

"In *Copycat* Phil shows us a better way to pass on the life and ways of Jesus to others. He writes 'Being a copycat [of Jesus] is how you become you,' pointing us to the importance of picking up the life of Jesus from others around us and also passing on these traits to future generations. This is how God's kingdom moves forward in power."

Matt Brown
Evangelist, Founder of Think Eternity
Author, *Awakening*

Copycat

Finding Our Originality

PHIL ZARNS

Urban Loft Publishers | Portland, Oregon

Copycat
Finding Our Originality

Urban Loft Publishers
2034 NE 40th Avenue #414
Portland, OR 97212
www.urbanloftpublishers.com

ISBN-13: 978-0692554289

Made in the U.S.A.

Cover artwork: Nathan Schroeder and Phil Zarns.

Table of Contents

List of Illustrations

Dedicated to my family
... my greatest opportunity to learn

"And you should imitate me, just as I imitate Christ."
Paul the Apostle
1 Corinthians 11:1

Foreword

by Bobby Loukinen

I met the author during his junior year in high school, and early in our friendship I sensed there was something special about this young man. A friend of his who attended our church invited him to attend our church's youth group one Wednesday night.

He was an intelligent kid who was very popular in our local high school. He was a good student and possessed a very quick wit and a keen sense of humor. I wish I could tell you an amazing story about the very first time I met him, and how God had spoken to me about this world-changer who was standing before me, and how I saw such incredible potential in his life. That wasn't how it all happened.

The first time I met Phil I noticed a confidence in how he handled himself. Some would mistake that for cockiness, but I saw it as more of a "you can't tell me what to do unless you convince me you are right" attitude. I remember talking with my wife about this new kid who had been at youth group that night and how he might be trouble. It was early in our youth ministry, so I wasn't sure how this was going to play out.

Soon after I arrived as the new youth pastor, I heard that Phil was a really good guitar player, so I invited him to be part of our worship band as a way to get him involved. The tip proved right; he wasn't just good, he was really good, bordering on great. Phil would be on stage with the worship band every week playing worship songs he had never heard before and doing them quite well. He would occasionally throw in some shredding between verses and added some flare to a rather boring band of musicians.

The more time I spent around Phil, the more I was impressed with him. He wasn't that defiant high school guy like I had labeled him right away; rather, he was a pretty sincere kid trying to find his way in life. Then it happened, our first conflict.

In the mid-nineties, secular music was viewed very differently than it is today. It was just a few years after the Christian world had spent so much time and energy pointing out the "evils" of rock music and had burned most of its albums, so much so that the cassette tape craze had taken off. At the church, the new superstar of the worship band was starting to pose a real potential problem to the newly arrived youth pastor (me). He would routinely wear his favorite rock band shirts while playing on our worship team. There he would be, playing some riff during a classic worship song that speaks about "giving thanks to God" in his favorite Pink Floyd shirt. I realized I had a problem.

My first thought was to tell him he could no longer play in our band because of his choice of T-shirts. But I knew that wouldn't sit too well with him, so I did nothing about it for awhile. I put the issue to prayer, and I believe God gave me a win-win. I approached Phil the next Wednesday night after youth group and tactfully addressed the situation. I explained that this week's Led Zeppelin shirt was cool, but I wasn't too sure that it fit into what I was trying to teach the kids in the youth group about worship. Worship is about being pure before the Lord and expressing ourselves to Him, and I wasn't too sure that Robert Plant and the boys held the same opinion. So I pitched the solution God had given me. I asked him to come back next week with whatever shirt he wanted to wear, but during the worship time to bring a buttoned-down shirt to put over the band shirt so that it would not distract people from worshipping God.

The conversation went much better than I had rehearsed it in my head, and he willingly accepted my suggestion. Not that it was a pivotal point in his relationship with the Lord, but rather a pivotal point in his relationship with me. Years later, he admitted to me that the rock music T-shirts were a test, and had I responded like I had initially wanted to, that might have closed the door on our friendship, our working relationship, and potentially his relationship with the Lord.

After our near-disaster confrontation, I don't remember having any more conflicts with Phil the rest of the semester, and we starting getting along great. I had inherited a strong tradition in our church for students to attend a summer Bible camp, and Phil agreed to attend, not knowing what he was getting himself into. I think he went because his friends were telling him about how fun it was and that there were hundreds of pretty girls there rather than anything that might help him grow in his relationship with Christ.

The first night of camp, I saw God change Phil's world! He has never been the same since. The second night was even better, and by the last night of camp, God had called him into full-time ministry and put a call of missions upon his life. In twenty-four years of ministry, I have never seen someone change so radically in just one week of summer camp. Phil came back to our small town totally and completely changed. He came back not content to sit and let things just happen; instead, he was determined to make things happen.

He felt like he was on a "mission from God" to change his high school, and for the next year I witnessed him taking that calling very seriously. His leadership brought our See You At The Pole prayer rally to a whole new level. The campus Bible study at the high school had never gone better, and he would fearlessly and unashamedly talk about what God had done in his life. Phil had a profound impact on his high school his senior year because he had met Jesus in more than just a religious way. It was in a very powerful personal way, and it started to affect every area of his life.

During the summer between his senior year of high school and college, Phil joined me on a mission trip to Guatemala. Something I was very impressed by was his refusal to ask anyone else for money to help fund his trip. He had chosen to pay for the entire trip out of his own bank account. He was determined to make this the very best trip it could be because it had cost him so much personally. While on that trip, I saw him start to excel in the gifts God had given him: from playing his guitar, to singing and performing in the dramas, to speaking publicly in front of thousands of students about his faith in Christ and how it had caused such a radical change in his life.

After that trip, it was hard to believe this was the same kid I had met only a year and a half before. I knew there was something different about Phil … and now I was starting to see that it was God's hand upon his life. God had given him a purpose in life and a dream. This book is a partial fulfillment of that dream.

I have seen firsthand over the past twenty years of Phil's life a passion for his relationship with the Lord. I also have seen in him an intense desire to share the life-giving message of Jesus Christ to everyone he comes in contact with. One of the best ways that Phil has discovered to do this is to disciple students and adults he has the privilege to minister to and walk with in his faith journey.

For Phil, this message of "Imitate me as I imitate Christ" is not just something written in a book. It is a lifestyle I have seen him implement over the years we have been friends. It all started for Phil by powerfully meeting Jesus, much like Paul did on the road to Damascus. And it continues today in the ministry to which God has called him and his family in Stockholm, Sweden.

Phil's transformed life is living proof of what a meeting with Jesus can do, and I hope this book brings you closer to the God who radically changed his life!

Bobby Loukinen
Youth Pastor, Home Missionary in student and overseas mission

Preface

Almost everything you will read in this book has been written about before. This is a collection of ideas that have steered our civilizations for thousands of years ... rather old ideas. Honestly, new ideas are few and far between these days. That said, I hope to show a gateway that has been long forgotten, or at least ignored as a foundational part of each of us.

I will make no excuses. I have wondered if I was qualified to produce a book about this subject. Shortly after consulting some friends who offered kind words, I began writing.

The writing comes from moments of observation, both myopic and inspired. I've invested much thought into this book for three years before daring to scrawl out a single idea.

In each chapter I'll relate a scientific idea to the question at hand. I hope this is not too nerdy for you.

A Brief Roadmap

Chapter 1: Copycat – Relies on the idea that we are hardwired to be copycats.

Chapter 2: Mimicry – Brings a scientific focus of how mimicry strengthens nature, business, and relationships.

Chapter 3: Process – A process of development is placed before each of us to grow through learning and copycatting others through difficulty.

Chapter 4: Mentor – Finding or being a mentor, and the characteristics that make a great shepherd. We become who we serve.

Chapter 5: Setup – Inspired by the Holy Spirit, the Old Testament prophets and kings operating in transitions of sin, blessing, and leadership. Potential energy is just waiting to be released.

Chapter 6: Spark – How Jesus Christ opens up the global opportunity for others to copycat him!

Chapter 7: Reputation – Once we are set in motion, a chain reaction of life events speeds us into an original reputation built by God.

Chapter 8: Transfer – A challenge for us to pass along what we have learned so more copycats can experience an original life in Christ.

Chapter 9: Atmosphere – The gift of consequence learned from an early age blesses the future of your family and the church.

Appendix: Be a Copycat - Express Yourself – Take steps to write your own story.

Thank you for reading, and for giving me some of your precious minutes in order to share these thoughts.

Phil

Acknowledgements

The initial outline to this book was scrawled out during a flight to Dallas. The draft was written three years later over a period of two months. Late nights and early mornings were dedicated to developing the draft. No matter how hard I worked on *Copycat*, one fact remains: Without the following people, this book never would have seen the light of day.

To my wife, friend, and partner-in-ministry, Katja: Your support, drive, integrity, and passion keep me honest. I could never ask for a stronger advocate for my work. I can always count on you for ideas and guidance. Thank you for contacting the publisher to get the ball rolling on *Copycat*. Your valuable encouragement is that I should never settle for quick work.

To my children, Ben, Matilda, and Max: Your care, love, nonstop creativity, perseverance, overwhelming joy, and honesty are life to me. Thank you for the ride we are on together!

To Michael: Thank you for the conversation that put my outline to work. "Why wouldn't you write this?"

To Matt, Joseph, the Aarons, and the Chrises: Thank you for your friendships, your suggestions and your test reading skills.

To Sean and Urban Loft Publishers: Thank you for taking a chance on me. Your vision and focus deeply resonate with me.

To editors Frank and Jill: I don't want to write too much here, as you may find an error. To edit is divine. Thank you for helping to redeem my work.

To my agent, Les Stobbe: Thank you for asking the right questions and for your guidance.

To the Brainy Bunch: You know who you are. Thank you for working alongside me, pushing me to do "good work" without even realizing your influence.

To my dog, Yoda Minnesota: Thank you for the hundreds of walks, rain or shine, that we took together. Through that time with you, the ideas kept coming.

To my family near and far: Thank you, Mom and Dad, for believing in me. I love you.

To my Creator: Thank you for life, creativity, and the opportunity to copycat you.

Chapter 1

Copycat

*Copycat—one who imitates or adopts the behavior
or practices of another.*[1]

And you should imitate me, just as I imitate Christ.[2]

Think of your favorite coffee shop. Yes, you know the one. As you open the door, the aroma of the freshly ground beans fills your senses. You step to the counter and order a nonfat macchiato, a triple-shot cappuccino, or a hazelnut latte with a dash of cinnamon. Regardless of your choice, you experience a feeling of belonging in your order as they call you by name to claim your custom-crafted drink.

I hate to break it to you, but five hundred thousand other people ordered the same drink as you this morning. You are part of a greater whole. Americans alone down one hundred million cups of coffee everyday, not to mention the massive 2.25 billion cups consumed worldwide each day. Tea drinkers? They drink two billion cups, a shade less than their coffee counterparts.

---

[1] *Merriam-Webster Dictionary*, 2005.

[2] 1 Cor. 11:1.

Although we wake to the same sunrise, out of billions of people, no two of us are exactly alike. We each have distinctive height and body shapes, hair colors, eye colors, and skin hues that combine to form our own unique selves. It is my share of these differences that make me who I am. We don't necessarily align in terms of style and taste, either. I might like a certain musical style, while you might find that choice disconcerting. Our preferences of movie genres, restaurants, automobiles, mobile phones, even our choice of computers, make us feel like a one-of-a-kind individual. We define ourselves by the choices we make.

Yet we aren't really all so different.

Trends

There was a hot musical debate during the 1960s—are you a Beatles fan or a Rolling Stones fan? Whoever you chose, you took a side, not just personally, but along with a large part of America and Britain. Even if you didn't care for either band, you then joined the millions of people who were completely indifferent. By having your own taste, or choosing not to choose, you became part of a demographic.

Tattoo shops started popping up left and right in the United States during the 1990s. By 2010, approximately fifteen thousand were legitimate businesses, turning America on to the art. Today, 20 percent of Americans have a tattoo somewhere on their bodies. The number one reason people get tattoos is to express their originality. What started as a sign of rebellion turned into a fad, developing into a long-term trend as fifty million tattoos of all shapes and sizes emboss people's skin. If you choose not to get inked, you are a part of a shrinking demographic. Those people not getting tattoos are becoming the rebels.

Trends can appear as short-term fads or long-term sociological changes. How we drink our coffee, where we drink it, and how it is made, all come into play in how this trend develops.[3] Great moments can originate because of a few specific factors that were ignited by a special situation.[4] Whether something remains a fad or whether the culture adopts it, trends reveal that we are all very much alike. As rivers of change, these likenesses flow through every part of our lives.

People find the most recent trends through a previously neglected button on our keyboards, the #hashtag. Hashtags and social media allow people to share their interests across the Internet, finding new ways to group together. One click on a hashtag on Twitter or Facebook, like #ilovechocolatecake, pulls up tweets and statuses of people from all over the globe who share a love of chocolate cake.

What about trends that are not so vain? The Folding@home project devotes itself to finding new ways of folding microscopic proteins to help fight disease. Sony PlayStation includes an option to complete computations for the Folding@home project while the console is not in use. More than fifteen million PlayStation owners have donated their machines, and more than one hundred million hours of computation helped to advance the medical research. It is amazing what people can accomplish when they copy the examples of other people.

On another level of selflessness are the innumerable groups dedicated to social justice, such as those focused on stopping the

[3] Vejlgaard, *Anatomy of a Trend*, loc 499.

[4] Gladwell, *The Tipping Point*, 29.

sex-trafficking of women and girls. A21 and Project Rescue are rallying to stop this horrific trend that has existed for centuries and are starting a trend of freedom in its place.

How do trends thrive and continue? It's simple. When one person does something, another person copies him or her. Whether good or bad behavior, another person can imitate every word we speak and action we take. People follow their parents' behavior, buy the same brand of grill as their neighbors, visit similar vacation spots, and copy the type of shoes other people wear. The list goes on and on. Our personalized expressions are not as uncommon as we may realize. We become a part of a trend by simply copying someone else. One of the strongest challenges in the Bible is, "Imitate me, just as I imitate Christ."[5]

Our Need to Be Noticed

So why do we want to have customized coffee and personalized music playlists? We already know that we like these things, but is there a deeper reason why we need something made just for us? By the way, that barista just called your name!

Another way to examine this question is to look at the formula for almost any '80s romantic comedy: a story about the girl, her jerk boyfriend, and the misunderstood nerd. The plot is set, and then there's a montage set to a song by Richard Marx. By the end of the movie, the nerd gets noticed by the girl, and the boyfriend is humiliated in front of the whole school, tarred and feathered. Which character do we associate with the most?

---

[5] 1 Cor. 11:1.

Inside each of us is a longing to be noticed. Whether it is having our name called out at the coffee shop or getting the girl or guy in the end, we want to feel like we *matter*. In 1943, Abraham Maslow, an American psychologist, introduced this concept in his hierarchy of human needs: (1) physiological, (2) safety, (3) love and belonging, (4) esteem, and (5) self-actualization. When we are secure in knowing we are loved and belong, we feel we matter as we are recognized in a deep, meaningful way. The top floor of Maslow's hierarchy of needs is self-actualization, or fulfilling our potential. This is the step at which people simply become who they are meant to be! We want to reach beyond just fitting in, beyond just feeling good about ourselves. We want to do something that fulfills our hearts and is, in totality, original.[6]

Together

We need to learn from other people. In the course of his military career, George Washington had been a prisoner of war while at other times dominating in battle. All of this happened before he became the President of the United States. Neil Armstrong spent years in the Navy as a test pilot for experimental aircraft before he ever set foot on the moon. Both Washington and Armstrong had hundreds of thousands of people who supported them on their ventures. Both Washington and Armstrong worked in relationship with, learned from, and were propelled forward by colleagues who helped them to develop into the leaders we know them to be today.

---

[6] Maslow, "A Theory of Human Motivation," 382.

Like these two incredible people, we learn from relating to other humans, creating bonds with each other, and by then creating environments where others can belong and thrive. They had to learn their skills from someone else. All that they used was learned from someone else.

Maslow was correct. To encourage each other in the first place, we need to be together. To be together, we need to be accepted into a form of belonging and loved. Most everyone who pioneers, produces, or discovers something of great importance shares a strong form of connection and appreciation to those around them. So why would we try to live otherwise? With the help of mentors, individuals can become part of the process of learning while setting new trends that change lives. Not only would we be original, but also we could live out our potential alongside others.

It's as if we were meant to be copycats.

The Ugly

The term "copycat" first appeared in literature during the late 1800s as a term describing someone who "writes anything that has already been printed."[7] On a more notorious note, authorities in the mid-1900s used the label copycat to describe murderers who imitated one another. Clearly, being called a copycat was anything but a compliment.

Imagine a kid peeking at his friend's paper midway through a math test. If caught, the friend would harshly whisper, "*Copycat!*" If the friend said it loud enough, the teacher would perk up, and the cheating kid would receive an "F," sitting in the

---

[7] Harrison, *Bar Harbor Days*, 96.

corner with one less friend. A study at Yale University asserts that once children reach age five, they will recognize and attempt to stop anyone from copycatting them.[8]

The meaning of the term has become much broader over time to include copying another person's *behavior*. In essence, if you name an action, it can be copied. As a culture, we have decided that copying another person is bad, even frowned upon. How do we then explain fashion trends? In the world of teenage fashion, trends come and go with each passing year, month, or week with increasing creativity. One piece of fashion that continues to be cut and copied is jeans. According to a source who works in clothing trends in Scandinavia, most casual clothing brands all have strong denim lines.[9] Although they are copycats of each other, each pair of jeans is worn in so many different ways. Pinning jeans at the lower cuff recalls the trend current in 1992, while wearing a looser fit pays homage to the early 2000s. Tight, skinny jeans bring to mind the late '10s. Jeans will be alive and well in some form in the 2020s as well. Time will tell which form and to which degree of constriction our jeans will become.

The Bad

If the same cheating kid from the previous example continued being a copycat, he would find that the consequences of his behavior get worse in high school. If he still doesn't learn his lesson, the papers he would try to write at university, using keyboard shortcuts Ctrl-C, Ctrl-V, would lead to a more serious

---

[8] Olson, "No Fair, Copycat!" para. 4.

[9] Vuorinen, in discussion, May 2013.

accusation—plagiarism. An ever-growing number of websites and agencies devote themselves to stomping out plagiarism from a very young age. One of the websites warns copycats, "These aren't your thoughts or ideas."[10] The core of plagiarism is to fail to give credit to the original creator of the text.[11] We understand how trends develop—people copy other people. Unfortunately, these copying trends can be negative. So how do people start positive trends? When is it good to copycat? The answer lies within our own family structures.

The Good

Summer vacation had finally arrived. Our rented country home sat on a hill overlooking a valley with horses freshly set to pasture each morning. From our breakfast table, we watched as the dawn caused the hills to glow all around.

In one corner of the house sat an untuned piano.

My daughter had been plinking on the keys since we'd arrived. On one particular morning, she was trying out the small parts of Bach and Beethoven she remembered from school.

Out of the blue, my wife stepped to the piano. "I can teach you a song...."

"Really? You don't play piano," I said, surprised from across the room.

My daughter could hardly sit still. "Okay! Teach me!"

I had never seen my wife sit down at a piano, ever. She situated herself on the right, daughter on the left.

---

[10] KidsHealth.org, "What Is Plagiarism?" para. 3.

[11] Office for Research Integrity, "Plagiarism of Ideas," para. 1.

Heart-and-soul, ba-da-da-da-da-dah, Some-other-words, ba-da-da-da-da-dah, deedum, da-da-da-da-da-da, da-da, da-da, da-da, dah ...

There she went, playing the piano. After working through the melody together a few times, they switched spots. Katja, my wife, began to play the rolling rhythm with both hands to the melody she had just shown my daughter. *Da-da da-da, da-da da-da, da-da da-da, da-da da-da ...*

Then came the moment when they played melody and harmony. *Heart-and-soul ...*

I stared across the room at my wife, whom I thought I knew everything about! Katja played, Matilda listened. By the end of fifteen minutes, Matilda played and Katja listened. The sweetest moment didn't occur when they played separately, but when they played together.

Matilda ran with it. Over and over, she practiced each part, calling Katja back occasionally to help her figure out the rhythm and timing.

By the end of the day, Matilda could play the interchangeable parts with ease. Now she had a new song to teach someone else. What smiles they shared!

Results

Copycatting can be good. My daughter copied my wife's actions at the keyboard, didn't she? I think everyone can agree that what happened was positive. My daughter was being a "copycat" of her mom. To this day, I can ask my daughter to play "*Heart and Soul,*" and she'll sound it out, note for note. Matilda heard something she liked and followed the same movements as her mom. Someday she will teach her own daughter the same tune. Mimicking others seems to be the way that we learn, doesn't it?

So what motivates human behavior to copy in the first place? Consider Matilda. The catalyst for her to copycat her mom's behavior was the drive for ... drumroll please ... results. The reason people copy, mimic, or learn anything for that matter is so they might some day do something they watched someone else do. To a greater extent, the reason we learn is to do something pioneering, pushing the boundaries of what we already know and see. We want to find the beginning point of the undiscovered, to accomplish something entirely original.

The reason anyone learns to play a song is to make music. Hours of practice might seem boring, but time with an instrument only sharpens people to perform better.

The reason for a kid to cheat on his test or copy someone else's work is so he will get a good score. Everyone wants to get an "A" on a test, right? Not only do university graduates discover wild new ideas, but they earn higher annual salaries on average. Taking shortcuts via plagiarism might render the results they want, but the benefits would come at a moral cost. In both the example of my copycat daughter and the cheating test-taker, they copied the ideas of another to get the results they wanted. We're copycats by nature, because of a need to do things well. Yet notice this: Katja's mentoring relationship with our daughter became stronger because of their copycatting. The cheating test-taker gained nothing more than a better test score served with a steaming pile of guilt.

Copying is part of the learning process, and by removing this process, we would hamstring even the smartest kids. One must learn how to walk before she can run. The Bible reveals that God only wants the best for his children,[12] and he helps them on their way. So how do we know when it is okay and legally acceptable to copycat?

If we are destined to be copycats, we should begin with giving credit where it is due. During the Academy Awards ceremonies, the people thanked most by the winners were as follows: (1) the Academy, (2) spouses, (3) mother and father. Thankfully, the parents weren't the least mentioned.[13] In fact, mom and pop are the world's most powerful trendsetters to a child.

If the copycat cheater scored 100 percent on his test, he would get the "A" he was looking for. If his teacher put him on the spot and asked if the work was his own, would he give credit to his neighbor? If he told the truth, he would admit he plagiarized. But copycat cheaters claim all the credit for themselves.

Ask my daughter Matilda how she learned to play piano, and she'd point directly and proudly at her mom. Positive copycatting passes credit on to the people who deserve it.

The Bible centers on someone who selflessly passed along all credit to his own Father. Jesus always pointed people toward his Father.[14] He came to earth and copied humankind's *homoiōma*

---

[12] Matt. 7:11.

[13] Collins, Academy Awards, para. 3. God, on the other hand, has been thanked around 15 times out of 775 speeches.

[14] Matt. 5:16, 5:45.

("likeness" in Greek), teaching people that they can trust in the same source he trusted. Only an unlimited source can power this life-giving faith that will last for generations to come. When people copycat Jesus's example, they do just as he did and in so doing point to the original author. As believers begin to trust God, he becomes their mentor. He leads his followers through the process of life, directing and inspiring each person to mentor and care for others.[15]

Parents must pass on the wisdom, values, and traditions they have collected throughout their lives. Generations are counting on this.

How We Learn

The noise of a crowded delivery room, the blinding lights in our eyes, and the shocking cold all rush over our senses the moment we are born. All we can say in response: "WAAAAAHHHH!" Yet in just four months, babies begin to develop the capacity to copy the sounds they hear and the movements they see. They even begin smiling and frowning at this stage.[16] How people learn is an expansion of this process. If they're close to their parents, kids will learn how to act and react by watching and copying their actions and reactions. My kids have even learned to have mini road rage!

Copying another's behavior is the way we learn.[17] These are incredible moments for young parents and their babies, because

[15] 2 Tim. 3:16-17.

[16] Centers for Disease Control and Prevention, "Learn the Signs, Act Early," para.3.

[17] PBS, "Babies Are Natural Copycats," para.3.

whole rivers of learning start to flow from parents to children. They create new trends.

Kids also can learn from other kids. They can, for instance, copycat playing with fire, handling large knives, or jumping off tall things. Kids will try almost anything they see someone else do. Many of you reading this have been *that* kid. Congratulations to you and your parents—you survived!

When my daughter chose to start playing "*Heart and Soul*" by herself instead of following my wife's lead, she took responsibility for carrying on the tune. This transition between generations is an idea that comes directly from the Bible, and it is instilled in life itself. God unlocked the potential energy in his people by giving them his Spirit.

That same Spirit in Jesus Christ, was passed on to his followers. God was going global, baby! Before that, he had whispered his message, but now he would shout out loud that message and carry it to the edges of the earth.

Parents need to have the hope that their children's lives will be better lives than theirs. Any leader worth following would want this for their disciples as well. After playing "*Heart and Soul*" for hours, there was a moment when Matilda dared to set her fingers outside of the pattern she learned from her mother, to play a new song. Children do not just mirror their parents' behavior, but they can be creative and proactive in trying new things themselves and setting new trends.[18] God has hardwired humans to have children, passing along their experiences to them and so on. The copycat process begins all over again with each generation.[19]

---

[18] Bandura, *Social Cognitive Theory*, 15.

[19] Gen. 1:27.

We live in a world of people who are noncommittal, who don't like to be defined by labels, and who desire to be original. I want to challenge you as we discover some truths in the following chapters:

- How people learn by mimicking others
- How each person experiences a refining process
- How people can benefit from mentors
- How people can unlock their potential by being copycats
- How people can pass on their own original experiences

Being a copycat is not a path to becoming a clone.
Being a copycat is how you become you.

Copycats and Jesus

Christians face the challenging task of changing[20] to become like Jesus Christ in how he served others. Copycatting Jesus sets before us a process of following his teachings so that we will know what truth in this world is, and so we can show others who he is and how to trust him.[21] He asks us to trust in mentors who have gone before us, to be prepared to do "even greater things,"[22] and to pass on this way of life to our children[23] and others.[24] It turns out that being a copycat is how we become original.

---

[20] Phil. 2:7.

[21] Eims, *The Lost Art of Disciple Making*, 62.

[22] John 14:12.

[23] Deut. 6:7.

[24] Matt. 28:19.

Study Questions:

1. Can you remember a time when you copied the example of another as a child? Who did you copy this week?
2. Jesus is described as a Servant in Philippians 2. As we copy Jesus, what internal struggles might we face in following his example? What external challenges could we face?
3. When is it okay to copy the example of someone else? When is it not okay?

Chapter 2

Mimicry/Mimesis

Imitation is the sincerest form of flattery.[1]

One of the most widely embraced music groups of all time, the Beatles, broke their own songwriting formula after each and every song they recorded.[2] Not only was this a way to stay creative and original, but it also threw off the hundreds of bands who copycatted their guitars, clothes, boots, and haircuts in the 1960s.

The Rolling Stones released "As Tears Go By" four months after the Beatles released "Yesterday."[3] Even though the Stones recorded the hit a year and a half before the Beatles' song, their management wanted to piggyback on the success of the Beatles. Interestingly, both recordings shared glaring similarities, right down to the number of instruments, the vocalists, and the song arrangement.[4] Who copied whom?

Although the Beatles got a recording contract first, the debate goes on even today about how the Rolling Stones'

---

[1] Colton, *Lacon*, 114.

[2] Wegren, *Beethoven to Beatles*, December 1995.

[3] *Rolling Stone*, "*Rolling Stone*'s Top 10 Beatles Songs of All Time," para. 8.

[4] McMillian, *Beatles vs. Stones*, loc. 2352.

management purposefully copied the album cover designs of each Beatles album. The Stones' releases would then hit the shelves a few months later. A myriad of copycat bands popped up during the 1960s, mimicking not only the Beatles, but the Stones as well.

The art of mimicry is to imitate an idea, event, or invention to get a result.[5] In some cultures *mimicry* is deemed a negative term, while *mimesis* may define a more direct approach to change via deliberate imitation. Regardless, mimicry and mimesis refer to the art of being a copycat. In the case of the music industry, the ultimate goal is to sell albums, for bands to tour, and for fans to buy overpriced T-shirts. Turn on most pop music radio, and you're bound to hear copycats copying other copycats. Listening audiences just keep eating up the same stuff. Money and fame are impressive catalysts to get people to copycat others. What if the stakes were a bit higher, however? What about copying something else simply to survive?

Beautiful Butterflies

Copycats in the animal kingdom are split into two main classes, Batesian and Müllerian. Batesian mimicry happens when an animal that can be eaten imitates a similar animal that predators know is toxic. Müllerian mimicry happens when two similarly toxic species benefit from each other's presence in avoiding being eaten.

Scientists have understood monarch and viceroy butterflies to be Batesian in relationship, that is that the tasty viceroy was avoided because of its similarity to the bitter monarch. Their

---

[5] *Merriam-Webster Dictionary*, 2005.

near-identical wing patterns warded off predators from both species. Per experimentation, scientists used to believe that the viceroy was the copycat and the monarch was the model. This was widely accepted as fact in the scientific community. Ritland and Bower's groundbreaking findings[6] show that both butterflies taste incredibly bad to birds. Studies show that the previously tasty viceroy might have developed to become as toxic as the monarch.[7] This means that the butterflies are not an example of a Batesian relationship, but instead an example of a Müllerian relationship. The viceroy mimicked the taste of the monarch! Whether it be a new food source that caused this to happen remains to be understood. Yet out of the need to survive, these butterflies suggest that a copycat could not only mimic something else, but it could come to co-develop with the leading example. As the saying goes: fake it until you make it.

Butterflies mimic each other in ways that will ensure that both species survive. Sometimes two things can resemble each other so closely that it's incredibly difficult to tell them apart.

Humans

In order to test their physical limitations, humans have imitated their surroundings. Copying birds coasting on the breeze, people built airplanes that roar over the oceans. They caught and examined fish and built submarines that have similar ballast and pressurized air containers. They may have fallen from the sky and sunk to the depths many times in the process, but people continue to copycat their surroundings.

---

6 Ritland and Brower, "The Viceroy Butterfly Is Not a Batesian Mimic," 497.

7 Gamberale-Stille, "Feature Saltation and the Evolution of Mimicry," 809.

However successful we have been at copying animals, people are perhaps best at copying each other. By copycatting their parents, children learn how to eat, brush their teeth, and talk to others. Studies show that when we find something to be a positive experience, we copy that behavior.[8] As one person mimics another, the social interaction between the mimicker and mimickee establishes a greater bond between the pair.[9] In short, people grow closer in relationship when they copy each other. The deal breaker to this way of learning is when people outwardly show they have self-absorbed pride. Research concludes that when we sense pride in others, we will distance ourselves from them.[10] It seems that people are more likely to mimic humble people than prideful people.

Let's jump back to the beginning of the chapter. Can we find the mimicry evident in the Beatles and butterflies anywhere else?

The Cola Wars

"Coke is it!"

"You've got the right one, baby!"

"The Real Thing."

"The Choice of a New Generation."

These slogans from Coca-Cola and Pepsi have helped to pour millions of gallons of bubbling soda into frosty mugs for well over a century. The most popular question regarding these two products is of course, "Coke or Pepsi?"

---

[8] PBS, "Babies Are Natural Copycats," para. 3.

[9] Stel and Vonk, "Mimicry in Social Interactions: Benefits for Mimickers, Mimickees, and Their Interaction," 321.

[10] Dickens and DeSteno, "Pride Attenuates Nonconscious Mimicry," 7.

Both brands have had their failures. Pepsi filed for bankruptcy twice in the earlier part of the twentieth century, and New Coke failed to take off in 1985. Both Coca-Cola and Pepsi soon learned a principle from their marketing research that would change the way they communicated: superstars sell soda. Both brands have boosted their campaigns using celebrity help, hoping that stardom from the likes of Bill Cosby or Beyoncé might move more soda. Twenty years ago, Pepsi rewarded Michael Jackson with singed hair from a failed firework display during a commercial shoot. Michael Jordan reached for a bottle of Coke in E.T.-like fashion, their silhouettes hovering against a full moon. Even the companies' stock prices resemble each other.[11] Pepsi has been relentless at pumping up their image, trying to keep up with Coca-Cola and their brilliant use of the ubiquitous American icon, Santa Claus.

The most blatant act of mimicry between the companies is how their logos[12] parallel each other with their graphic redesigns. People can see waves in both brands' logos, as well as similar fonts and colors. One intriguing idea to note: research concludes that when a brand is a blatant rip-off of another, it does poorly in comparison to subtle imitations[13] of the same product. By the premise of this study, Pepsi should have failed long ago.

As the stronger brand, Coke has attracted a number of copycats to follow suit through the years. Competitors like RC Cola and Pepsi have benefited from the success of Coca-Cola,

---

[11] Dion Harmon et al., "Predicting Economic Market Crises Using Measures of Collective Panic," 6.

[12] Cnn Tees, "Coke vs. Pepsi: The Cola Wars."

[13] Van Horen and Pieters, "When High-Similarity Copycats Lose and Moderate-Similarity Copycats Gain: The Impact of Comparative Evaluation," 90.

mimicking the company in butterfly-like Batesian relationship.[14] Pepsi initiated the Pepsi Challenge, a blind taste-test pitting the two sodas against each other. Now on the offensive, Pepsi grew even stronger by buying up restaurant and product chains to increase their products' availability to the public. By increasing their shelf space with a variety of products like Crystal Pepsi, Diet Pepsi, and Mountain Dew, Pepsi increased sales as they occupied more of the soda aisle in grocery stores.[15] Both companies even buy beverage coolers for convenience stores as long as they keep their shops healthily stocked with Coke or Pepsi, respectively. Pepsi had qualified itself to be in a power struggle with Coca-Cola. The metaphor in the Cola Wars had changed from "king of the hill" to "versus."

The soda companies' styles of copycatting moved from Batesian, in which Pepsi tried to convince the public that it was good enough to be in the same league as Coke, to Müllerian, in which both Coca-Cola and Pepsi co-evolved as soda brands. They are the butterflies of the beverage world. Hopefully they're not as poisonous! Both drinks became more competitive for the public's money. While their consumers may not have been rewarded with better products, they certainly were "rewarded" with more advertising.

Copycats can be so similar that they can displace "The Real Thing" as the real thing. We've discovered copycats in the animal world, music industry, social situations, even in our own refrigerators. Many would like to believe that in the most original space, the art world, that this phenomenon hasn't happened.

---

[14] Falkenstein, "A Batesian Mimicry Explanation of Business Cycles," para. 8.

[15] Danielson, "The Perfect Soda," 2013.

That Smile

"Mona Lisa, Mona Lisa, men have named you ..." crooned Nat King Cole through the muffled speakers in my dad's rusty old Chevy pickup long ago. Years later I would get to visit the original, the true *Mona Lisa* painting. Her portrait hangs in the Louvre Museum, where people from all over the world visit to catch a glimpse of the modest smile that graces *Mona Lisa's* face. The piece was smaller than I expected, placed in a room guarded by a security detail and wired to an alarm system. The theft of the painting itself in 1911[16] deepens our sense of intrigue regarding the *Mona Lisa*. Many say her smile hides something. The reason for her secret smirk may have been her knowledge of a twin painting. Named for the county where it was found at the beginning of the twentieth century, the Islesworth *Mona Lisa*[17] became the center of a debate. Was this masterpiece a copycat? They looked so similar scholars wondered which one was the original *Mona Lisa*.

Exhausting every single scientific and physical method of examination they could find, the Mona Lisa Foundation figured out that the Isleworth is actually the earlier original painted by Da Vinci himself, while its copycat counterpart, also painted by Da Vinci, hangs in the Louvre. You can't make this stuff up. I am equally interested in the possibility that this might explain Mona Lisa's smile. Giorgio Vasari, a sixteenth-century writer of the times, told of how Da Vinci would keep people around to entertain Mona Lisa so the smile would continue throughout the

---

[16] Stevens, "Spekphrasis: Writing About Lost Artworks; or, Mona Lisa and the Museum," 54-64.

[17] Mona Lisa Foundation, "Summary of Scientific and Physical Examinations."

painting process.[18] I suggest two reasons for the smile: I'm supposing that Da Vinci asked her to pose this way, all the while in her heart she considered it a privilege to have not one, but two, individual portraits produced of her as the subject. She was flattered by the opportunity to have her likeness copied.

Imagine the time and the patience it would take to create a likeness of something you yourself had already painstakingly created. What if a person's goal is not to make a one-of-a-kind original, but instead to create several copies that embody the artistry of the original model? They would certainly require altogether different mechanics. Creating a single copy is noble and impressive, but making multiple copies is divine.

Near-Perfect Copies, Every Time

Historically, people's need for a larger amount of copied documents has pushed forward technology as a whole. Chiseled stone slabs were God's chosen medium for Moses.[19] Clay and wax tablets then gave way to thinly-stretched animal skins. Soon these were replaced by woven papyrus prepared from the reeds of the Nile. Nearly three thousand years ago, the Chinese took innovation further and invented paper, which people now use to keep to-do lists of emails to respond to using the next evolution of making copies: the digital screen.

More than five hundred years ago, when people needed to copy a piece of information, monks would do the monotonous work of hand-drawing multiple texts.[20] Working smarter, they

---

[18] Rorimer, "The Mona Lisa," 223.

[19] Exod. 34:1.

[20] Owen, *Copies in Seconds*, loc. 212.

developed an assembly-line method of copying books in order to increase efficiency. One worker scrawled capital letters exclusively, while another wrote in each paragraph's text. Increased or decreased pressure from the quill, fatigue, and poor lighting all caused each copy to contain small differences.

In 1455, Johann Gutenberg, creator of the Gutenberg Bible, invented a mechanical method for movable type printing that could make multiple copies of the same document. One of the motivating factors for the creation of this invention was the legibility of the type versus the legibility of the handwritten work. Soon after the first iterations of the press started to produce, the current Pope took notice and praised the machine's work.[21] Technology had taken copycatting to a new level. Gutenberg produced not just copies of the Bible, but he made copies of the press itself. Book printing evolved, and periodical newspapers popped up across Europe.

Fast-forward to the twentieth century when chemical-, steam-, and electric-powered automation took the place of Gutenberg's press. As the global population grew, people's need for written material increased, once again challenging individuals to develop new ways to copycat documents.

No matter the method of printing, there have always been restrictions. Stephen King recounts from his early days of teenage journalism that his hectograph machine, "incubated and supported spore-like growths in the printing jelly … as if infected with a potentially fatal disease."[22] My parents' business used a mimeograph machine to burn carbon copies of invoices, and they frequently had to rest the machine when it overheated.

---

[21] British Library, "Gutenberg Bible: The Basics," para. 2.

[22] King, *On Writing*, loc. 407.

In the past, the hands of scribes cramped, and today's inkjet printers run out of ink all too quickly.

Chester Carlson test-drove a new copying concept in his own kitchen and developed xerography. He was in process to build the modern-day copier. He was looking for a new way to print better copies of documents with higher precision, accuracy, and speed. In 1921 he found the answer when Einstein won the Nobel Prize for his explanation of how photo electricity worked.[23] Carlson used that idea to create the Xerox machine. It was an invention that almost every office administration would be pressured to purchase. An original thought had become an original invention. Carlson made near-perfect copies, although his marketing claimed perfect copies.[24] Even his technologically superior copycat techniques had their limits. Have you ever experienced a copier paper jam?

After failures and successes leading to dead ends and fortunes respectively, people can make copies of virtually any document near to perfection. Mimicry, whether it is singing a song, producing a similar product, creating a picture-perfect painting, or printing a manuscript using a Xerox machine, people never seem to get *perfect* copies.

No matter how hard we try, perfect copies are impossible. In our pursuit of imitation, our airplanes have no feathers as birds do and our submarines are much larger than 99 percent of aquatic animals. We are in pursuit of a perfect copy of something.

---

[23] Owen, *Copies in Seconds*, loc. 1045.

[24] O'Connell, "Happy Birthday, Copy Machine!" para. 12.

Mimicry and Jesus

Paul writes about how we don't have to pretend to be like Jesus, but we can actually experience a transformational change through God's own Spirit,[25] becoming near-perfect copies or likenesses. We don't have to wear the same clothes as Jesus or grow a stubbly, grizzly beard. We don't have to fake it till we make it. For some, growing beards is impossible anyway! Would you want to slap on a fake smile, sharing fake love, while in your heart you don't care at all? Even those with terrible attitudes, if they will humble themselves, can experience community with others as we also can. By being around people who are the real thing, you might start to be real as well.

What matters to God is that we allow our hearts to become more like His.[26] Copying the humility of his Son[27] and loving our neighbors as ourselves in becoming more and more like Him. As we continue to follow Jesus, God's promise is that we will develop into near-perfect copies of the likeness of Jesus Christ.

Now we see things imperfectly, like puzzling reflections in a mirror, but then we will see everything with perfect clarity. All that I know now is partial and incomplete, but then I will know everything completely, just as God now knows me completely.[28]

---

[25] Rom. 8:14.

[26] Ezek. 11:19.

[27] Phil. 2:3.

[28] 1 Cor. 13:12.

Study Questions:

1. In what ways can you see mimicry in the news? In science? In education? In art?

2. What seems to be the motivational factor in each example of mimicker/mimickee from this chapter? Beatles/Rolling Stones? Butterflies? Pepsi/Coca-Cola?

3. Gutenberg became famous for copying the Bible with his printing press. We read of how he copied his copying machine. What would this development mean in regards to how many Bibles would then be printed? How could we learn from this example in regards to discipling others?

Chapter 3

Process

*We are either in the process of resisting God's truth
or in the process of being shaped and molded by his truth.*[1]

*This third I will put into the fire;
I will refine them like silver
and test them like gold.*[2]

After thousands of years of commercial transactions, the
most precious of commodities is still gold. There's no other metal
that has replaced its popularity in wedding bands, and its prices
on the commodity market continue to rise. To produce a nugget
of 99.999 percent pure gold, someone must crush a piece of ore,
grind it, rinse it with chemicals, and even heat it to 900 degrees
Celsius. People can use the finished product for jewelry, in
sensitive electronics, and even as micro-thin sheets for embossing
and decoration.

The art of Kintsugi uses gold powder to bond pieces of
broken pottery back together in a stunning technique that not
only shows the history of each fracture, but also gives the bowl a

---

[1] Stanley, *How to Listen to God*, 10.

[2] Zech. 13:9.

second purpose. Gold runs along each fault line not attempting to blend in, but shining unashamedly against the shattered pieces it now holds together. The beauty of Kintsugi is found in the process of breaking and rebuilding. As our faults and weaknesses get revealed through difficulty, we can target and strengthen those broken areas of our lives we once were ashamed of.

Newton

We all are on our way somewhere, according to of Sir Isaac Newton's First Law of Motion.

An object either remains at rest or continues to move at a constant velocity, unless acted upon by an external force.[3]

Yet sometimes, we might feel like "an object at rest." If there isn't a catalyst, there won't be any motion. When we feel uninspired, we will have no drive. We will have poor decisiveness, a lack of design and vision, and in the end, we will accomplish nothing. No catalyst, no result.

Reaching into a golf bag ready to tee off a round of golf, we grab the club known as the driver. Let's nickname this club "The Catalyst." This external force will get everything moving along. Place the ball on the tee. When we swing the driver … Boom, off the ball flies! When we are born, we are set into motion. One day in the future, we will each stop as the friction and gravity of age becomes the external force to place us at rest, eventually on or in the turf.

If uninspired and not in motion, we would need an external force, a *catalyst*, to move us along. We need the push of a single

---

[3] Newton et al., *The Mathematical Principles of Natural Philosophy*, loc. 967.

domino to cause the rest of our potential energy to react.[4] A catalyst motivates a person to send in his or her application to a university, to apply for a job, or to call someone for that first date. In a way, think of yourself as the ball, the tee is a situation who elevates us into position, and our catalyst is a mentor whom we can trust. Here comes the swing, Boom!

New Puppy

I own a dog named Yoda. The first day my family brought him home as a nine-week-old puppy, we sent out a picture of him to our family and friends, announcing that our new dog had arrived. A week later, had we found the energy, we would have sent out the same picture with one simple phrase—*FREE DOG.* Even though we had read much on welcoming a puppy into our family, we had no earthly idea how much work it would take to keep the puppy from using the Force all over our home. Our family of five had essentially just taken on the care of an infant. Our job was to lead him through the housebreaking process so he could fit into our family. Believe me, it felt like Dagobah.

We had to get this puppy into the groove of our family. We designed a schedule to take him on a walk outside every hour, and we did the work to make it happen. Through freezing rain and deep snow, we had to be relentless to teach Yoda when and where to do his business. We starting spacing out our walks to every two or three hours, and the accidents were few and far between. Our drive gave us the result we wanted—our puppy had learned the ways of the Force! We needed to be the catalyst to get Yoda moving!

---

[4] 1 Pet.1:3.

When I was twelve years old, I wanted to play guitar more than anything else in the world. The first time I heard a Stratocaster belting out blues on the radio, I knew I wanted to sound like *that guy*. My ever-supportive mom booked some classical guitar lessons for me at the St. Francis Convent, an unlikely setting for my classic rocker of a teacher, Paul. In that small side room across from the prayer chapel, he traced out a design for practice that I needed to follow to get the results I wanted. I became a copycat of him for awhile. Paul taught me all of the basics: how to hold a guitar, pick the strings, fret a note, listen for tone, and play to a metronome. Practice at home was painful. I literally played until my fingers bled. I worked hard to develop calluses, played through thousands of scale repetitions, and learned plenty of chords.

My process of learning the guitar was messy. I misplayed notes, my phrasing was off, and my timing was horrific. To me, I was the worst guitar player ever. I was so far from what I thought I would sound like after a year of practice. It was so discouraging to hit the wrong chord for the umpteenth time.

I needed to work even harder than I had ever imagined. Joining a couple of bands, I put the few skills I had figured out to use. Out of the furnace and into the fire. I played under vastly different music leaders, some more forgiving than others. The process was like a pressure cooker of learning. My weakness as a guitar player was changing for the *better*. Eventually, someone asked me to teach them what I had learned. I was a poor teacher at first, but I got better as time passed by. At each stage of learning, I purposefully needed to submit myself to time spent and effort invested in the process. What was the result? On a good day, if my hands, ears, and mind cooperate, some good music is made because of the process. I'm still hopeful to copycat that sound I heard on the radio so long ago.

Insanity

It has been said that insanity is doing the same thing over and over again expecting different results. Interestingly enough, discipline is doing the same thing over and over again expecting the same results. This is how people get good at something. If I copy a behavior enough times, a learned response will follow. Recent research shows that for people to learn behaviors to the point they become a habit, they must dedicate sixty-six days to doing the actions in order to attain automaticity.[5] Remember this statistic, guitar players. Better days are ahead! A conscious, willed action can become a part of our subconscious living through the process of discipline.

This process can be difficult, painful, and even stressful. But it's worth the struggle when we start to see the results of continually submitting to the process. There are four steps in each process: desire, decision, design, and doing. This process of discipline unfolds in an unlikely way through an engineer who would change the face of music forever.

Fender

Born in 1909 to meager beginnings, Leo Fender learned that he loved electronics. He worked plenty of odd jobs while getting his degree in electrical engineering. During his time at

---

[5] Lally et al., "How Our Habits Are Formed," 1007.

university, Leo discovered a *desire* to work with electronics that lasted his entire life. After graduation, he found himself sitting at a desk as an accountant for the State of California.[6] He earned a steady paycheck, which was an attractive situation as a newlywed, yet he found himself uninspired and stationary. All of his potential energy was at rest. Suffice it to say, he was not living in his sweet spot.[7] Sound familiar? Can you imagine being stuck in a rut, destined to a life of doing something that is anything but life-giving? Leo may resonate with you. You might just have to copycat his next *decision*.

Desire, Decide, Design, Do

Shedding his desk, he decided to start his own small business repairing radios. While not a financially sound decision, he would at least have passion for his work. Mr. Fender walked away from stability to establish that life is more than money. Little did he know that this process of following his passion would affect millions of people. He certainly had no clue that his last name would one day grace the headstocks of countless guitars played by leading musicians worldwide.

By the same token, following his internal desire came at a cost. His idealism collided with reality, and his desires widened when he needed cash as his business endeavor developed. His time as an accountant taught him one thing quite well—how to tell when too little money is coming home. After moving locations a few times and having his entire workshop wash away during a flood, Leo's Radio Repair found a permanent address.

[6] Fullerton, *Guitars from George and Leo*, loc. 141.

[7] Collins, *Good to Great*, loc. 1668.

The process of finding a permanent location resulted in steady business, paid bills, and a happy wife.

But his desire didn't let him rest for even a moment. After he decided to make the move to the new location, he noticed a new business opportunity. He started manufacturing his own guitar pickups for local guitarists. According to Les Paul of Gibson guitar fame, one thing about Leo was that he could "immediately discern the simplest method of doing whatever had to be done."[8] Leo found something not yet created and decided to learn something new.

Leo first learned how guitar pickups worked, and then *designed* his own prototypes. For some of us, this would take a month to figure out. For Leo, it was just a normal Tuesday. At the time, because of World War II, electrical components were scarce. Leo set extra time aside to scavenge for a specific type of enamel-coated wire used for the hundreds of windings of each guitar pickup. Daily he decided to push himself and his idea even further. Leo partnered with Doc Kaufmann, working late every night to create a simple slide guitar and amplifier to accompany his guitar pickups. Despite his full workload, Leo started dreaming again.

---

[8] Rock and Roll Hall of Fame, "Leo Fender Biography," para. 3.

The Telecaster

In working as a repairman, and being preoccupied with the problems of others, I was always able to see the defects in the design of an instrument which overlooked completely the need of its maintenance. If something is easy to repair, it is easy to construct. The design of each element should be thought out in order to be easy to make and easy to repair. – Leo Fender[9]

Leo wanted to produce a low-cost, easy-to-build guitar with parts that people could replace within a few minutes.[10] The design that he and new partner George Fullerton put together was the Broadcaster, later renamed the Telecaster. They designed prototypes, and trial and error refined the guitar to something that fit Leo's vision. After successful reviews by local guitarists, they cut patterns and cast dies to mass produce the finished product. They couldn't keep up with the demand for his altogether original invention. The process paid off! *Desire, decision, design,* and *do!*

As they produced multiple copies of each guitar part, its modular nature allowed them to be manufactured quickly with high quality control. The manufacturers could remove and replace necks, and they could swap bodies if they found any defects. Leo made a guitar with curves and lines that an engineer would love but that players who previously could not afford higher-priced instruments could now enjoy. Here's a fun fact: Although he dreamed up this incredible instrument, Leo hadn't learned to play the guitar!

---

[9] White, *Fender: The Inside Story*, 19.

[10] Fullerton, *Guitars from George and Leo*, loc. 239.

On the wall of my office hangs a copy of the original five-hole pickguard Telecaster. It is an incredibly comfortable and playable electric guitar. It reminds me of the process—of reparability, of change, of originality. It also reminds me that copycatting something through mass production can still deliver a product that people will love and value. Leo Fender's path to make the Telecaster began seventy years ago. Guitarists get to play one of the finest, most affordable instruments in the world as a result of one person's desire, decision, design, and doing.

Process and Jesus

Long ago a sacrifice was made for each of us. Jesus Christ's *desire, decision, design,* and *doing* made the greatest discovery available to all: a relationship with God himself.[11] Jesus teaches us that we can learn new skills, and even discover a truly original idea, when we submit to the process God sets out before us. When we trust in each other's God-given skills, we "become mature, attaining to the whole measure of the fullness of Christ."[12]

Romans 12:1-2 shows us a pathway set out to help change the way we think about things by repeatedly submitting ourselves to the process of applying God's word to our lives.

Therefore, I urge you, brothers and sisters, in view of God's mercy, to offer your bodies as a living sacrifice, holy and pleasing to God —this is your true and proper worship. Do not conform to the pattern of this world, but be transformed by the renewing of your

---

[11] John 3:16.

[12] Eph. 4:13.

mind. Then you will be able to test and approve what God's will is—his good, pleasing and perfect will.

When we live with renewed minds and hearts, we start a process of discipline, that transforms us, leading us to results that we didn't realize were possible. A life lived in the forgiving, caring, loving way of Christ is nothing less than original. When we allow God to be our catalyst, then our drive, decisions, design, and doing all take on the likeness of God himself.

True inventors must rely on the talent and knowledge that God gives them in order to see true results. – George Fullerton, business partner to Leo Fender[13]

Study Questions:

1. What process have you intentionally made yourself go through that has deeply affected you?
2. What is the difference between insanity and discipleship?
3. When we give our lives to God, he begins to transform our mind. What can we expect to happen once we begin the transformation? Who decides which pattern of life to follow?

---

[13] Fullerton, *Guitars from George and Leo*, loc. 244.

Chapter 4

Mentor

Whomever you serve, you will subconsciously become.[1]

If I have seen further, it is by standing on the shoulders of giants.[2]

"You Gotta Serve Somebody."[3] Although it was voted as the second-worst song in Bob Dylan's song catalog,[4] at least the title holds true! No matter the importance of our work, we will always serve *somebody*. When we wait tables, we serve the customer. In sports, we serve the coach. Drive a tank? We serve a military commander. There will always be a person a step higher than you at any time. Now, if you have to serve somebody, it would make sense to serve someone who you would want to be more like! Once you find your desire in life and find a process of discipline to achieve it, your next step is to find someone who can mentor you through it all. Mentors are those who have already walked the road you have chosen. After all, it was the outcomes of their own processes that attracted you to them in the first place!

---

[1] Ziemke, in discussion, May 2000.

[2] Sir Isaac Newton, in a letter to Robert Hooke.

[3] Dylan, "You Gotta Serve Somebody," 1979.

[4] Greene, "Readers' Poll," para. 1.

So *who* are you going to copycat? The greatest form of mentorship I've received came from two sources: my parents and Christian leadership. Remember, no matter how hard we try to copycat someone else, we will never be perfect copies ... and that is good!

Two examples of mentorship can be found in the Bible: generational mentors and leadership mentors.[5]

Generational Mentors

As a Christian believer, I've had the privilege of having mentors in my life who sacrificed for me and loved me. First and foremost, I learned how to live by watching my parents. *Toledoth*[6] is the Hebrew word for "generations." When the Old Testament (or Jewish Scriptures) was translated from Hebrew into Greek, the first book in the collection, *Toledoth*, became Genesis. From the New Testament, the book of Matthew traces the Hebrew family bloodline from Adam to Jesus. In that list of generations, fathers and mothers passed on traditions and beliefs to sons and daughters, and so on. Parents are our intended original mentors. I've learned to value what my mother taught me about studying, and what my father taught me about having a strong work ethic. I'm still not sure which of them gave me stubbornness! We don't have to look far for mentors to copycat.

[5] Zarns, "Transition Between Teenagers and Young Adults Within the Pentecostal Church of Sweden," 10-11.

[6] Marshall et al., *The New Bible Dictionary*.

Leadership Mentors

Moses, David, Elijah, Peter, Paul, not to mention Jesus Christ, were leaders/mentors famously written about in the Bible. As with the lineage of generations, so leaders have mentored other leaders. (We'll take a deeper look at this type of mentorship in the next chapter.) I have learned from many different mentors in my walk as a follower of Christ. My closest mentor and friend is my wife Katja. My kids, Ben, Matilda, and Max all teach me new things daily! Chronologically, in my Lutheran church it was Pastors Smith and Steffenson who taught me an incredible amount of Bible knowledge. Confirmation with these mentors taught me creeds and commandments, although I fought accepting the teaching. From Pastors Bobby and Keith I learned—and I'm still learning—how God changes lives. I can still remember verses I memorized in Bobby's discipleship class in 1994. Josh taught me how to be a friend, Travis taught me passion, Pastor Allen taught me how to stay faithful to my work. Reijo—patience; Bob—passion; Steve —conversation; Clarence—strength; Mark—joy; John— compassion; Matt—listening; Darin—decision making; Aaron – pastoring; Ryan and Jay—focus; Chuck—how to wait on God; Christopher—flexibility; Greg—trust; Tim—practicality; Chris —thought; Niklas—storytelling; Pelle—confidence; Anita— excellence; Nicklas—encouragement; Mattias—form ... and the list goes on and on! Some I copied more than others, but each helped me along the way. (We'll take a deep look at generational and leadership mentors in Chapter 5.)

Each one of these mentors had a quality about them that was meant to be copycatted. Whether they were my peers or my bosses, they all had the heart of a shepherd.

The Heart of a Shepherd

We're going to go to the Bible now and Psalm 23. This famous passage of Scripture is often read at funerals. Its calming words are just the thing we need in our time of grieving, setting the stormiest of hearts at ease. Yet when I read this passage apart from a funeral setting, I see an incredibly *active* picture of God painted in words by David, the shepherd-king.

> *The Lord is my shepherd;*
> *I have all that I need.*
> *He lets me rest in green meadows;*
> *He leads me beside peaceful streams.*
> *He renews my strength.*
> *He guides me along right paths,*
> *bringing honor to his name.*

He leads, he renews, he guides. A mentor, particularly one you will want to copycat, has the heart of a shepherd. Jim Brown, director of Exodus Ministries in Northern Ireland,[7] spent time in the hills of Romania learning from an actual shepherd on how to care for real sheep. The advice the shepherd shared went something like this: "To do this job, you have to care for the sheep, and you have to be with the sheep."

Caring for something or someone implies a close proximity. Being near to others in heart, soul, and mind is essential. A Skype call to someone across the world can transmit faces, but not an embrace. God so loved the world that he gave his Son,[8] who came to earth to seek out and be with the disciples—who were a salty bunch to say the least! Their lives, habits, and actions

---

[7] Brown, "Shepherd," 2012.

[8] John 3:16.

metaphorically smelled and sounded exactly as would a sheep pen. Because of Jesus's love, he chose to be near the stinky, loud mess that they were, and that we are. Baa-a-a-a-ah!

One of the challenges in being a shepherd is in enduring the monotony of watching the sheep. When distractions arise, mentors can be drawn away for any number of reasons. Jim's friend told a story of the shepherd who had chosen to leave the flock on the hills and walked to town to grab a pint. Once he returned from the pub, he found that three hundred sheep had been slaughtered, their bodies strewn out over the hills. Wolves had attacked while the shepherd was absent. Jesus, on the other hand, promises this about his proximity to us: "I am with you always to the very end of the age."[9]

Jesus calls himself the Good Shepherd in the Gospel of John.[10] He also says that his sheep know his voice, and that he calls them by name.[11] Amazingly, a study from the University of Cambridge found that sheep would actually answer when called by name,[12] although learning that takes time and repetition. There's something to process: How alike we are!

The Gospel of Matthew recounts a parable told by Jesus about a shepherd who left ninety-nine sheep in order to find the one that had gone roving. "If ... he finds it, truly I say to you, he rejoices over it more than over the ninety-nine which have not gone astray."[13] Jesus places an enormous amount of value on the action of the shepherd who went on a mission to find the one

---

[9] Matt. 28:20.

[10] John 10:11.

[11] John 10:3.

[12] Gray, "Sheep Are Far Smarter Than Previously Thought," para. 11.

[13] Matt. 18:13.

that was lost. Numbers are easy to understand; ninety-nine is larger than one. What Jesus wants to make clear is that *the one matters*. If *one* does not matter to a mentor, that person isn't fit to follow. We'll call this principle *the Rule of the One*. Jesus wraps up this passage perfectly: "… it is not the will of your Father who is in heaven that one of these little ones perish."[14]

Humility

The shepherd Jim had visited in Romania lived seasonally with the flock in a small hut on the side of the mountain. He kept close watch as much as sleep would allow. Mentors worth copycatting will look out for their sheep, expressing concern if they don't see them for a few weeks. A mentor with the heart of a shepherd takes on the Christlike humility found in Philippians 2:8, "He humbled himself and became obedient unto death." Andrew Murray expands this verse to say that, "Humility is the blossom, of which death to self is the perfect fruit."[15] Being and staying humble keeps a mentor centered on the needs of the weaker, the mentee.

I can explain this best by saying that Jesus is the ultimate example of humility. Despite possessing all power, he considered himself to be nothing on our behalf! Maybe you are a parent in the process of sacrificing your time, hobbies, and money so that your kids will have a better life. Jesus placed his own needs out of the way so that we might have a better life by following him. Like a child to a parent, Jesus wants us to choose him as mentor. There is always a risk that a mentee will not follow the leadership

---

[14] Matt. 18:14.

[15] Murray, *Humility and Absolute Surrender*, 45.

and guidance of a mentor. They may even push the patience and sacrifice back in their mentors' face, refusing to follow. The humility and forgiveness of Jesus Christ expresses itself through the character of a mentor who gives a second chance when it is needed most!

Skill

However, shepherds need to be more than good-hearted and humble. Wolves can still attack even the good-hearted. We see in Psalm 23:4 that like shepherds, mentors also need to be skilled in the use of the rod and the staff:[16]

Even when I walk
through the darkest valley,
I will not be afraid,
for you are close beside me.
Your rod and your staff
protect and comfort me.

The rod, in actuality, was a club used to beat down any predators that came close to the sheep. The staff was used to keep the sheep from straying, extending the reach of the shepherd. Get back here! A mentor's warnings can act in the same way. If we stray too far, a mentor will protect us by correcting our foolish mistakes. I wouldn't want a limp-wristed waif watching the sheep, would you?

But David said to Saul, "Your servant has been keeping his father's sheep. When a lion or a bear came and carried off a sheep from the flock, I went after it, struck it and rescued the sheep from

---

[16] Ellsworth, *Opening Up Psalms*, ch. 4.

69

its mouth. When it turned on me, I seized it by its hair, struck it and killed it."[17]

David knew the Rule of the One! The process of battling wild animals got him ready to save a nation. We would like to have mentors who are skilled as well as humble. Remember, a shepherd cares for the sheep and stays with the sheep.

Questions

The Western Church has experienced a mass exodus in the past few decades.[18] Why is that? There are a number of reasons, yet there's no specific answer anyone can pinpoint. What may have happened is: (1) Those who left the church had not taken responsibility to ask the questions they had on their hearts, while (2) equally, the mentors had not provided a space for dialogue or questions. It's a blaming game that we can get caught in. We need mentors in our churches who are humble and who are skilled in decisiveness. The sheep aren't responsible for the flock; that responsibility belongs to the shepherd.

The Latin word for "shepherd" is *pastor*, the modern name for clergy in many mainline and evangelical churches. Pastors come in all shapes and forms, from charismatic stage-pacers to quiet coffeehouse philosophizers. The heart of a shepherd can dwell in each pastor, as long as they remember the Rule of the One. We've seen that two important characteristics to look for in a mentor are humility and skill. How then is a mentor to hear

---

[17] 1 Sam. 17:34.

[18] Jaktlund, "Den Stora Kyrkflykten," para. 1. And Kinnaman, "Six Reasons Young Christians Leave Church," para. 4.

the unanswered questions that are compelling people to leave the church?

Active Shepherd

Proximity is a huge factor in figuring out how to diffuse the ticking time bomb of unanswered questions. A shepherd who cares for the sheep will be nearby! Mentoring one-on-one is a great opportunity to get any sort of dialogue initiated. My own research into different ways to mentor others had me looking for a Swiss army-knife technique of mentoring. Given the vast differences in shapes and forms of mentors, mentees, and situations, the method should be simple and hopefully theologically accommodating. Seeking God's Holy Spirit for guidance through prayer prior to any mentoring meeting is of the utmost importance. Without God's wisdom, decisiveness, and love, any model of mentoring becomes profoundly limited.

Let's consider three separate, yet related, attributes of a conversation: (1) Review the mentee's history, (2) review how current trends affect him or her, or (3) be ready with the understanding of biblical helps. This synthetic method developed by Richard Schreiter is a flexible way of combining all three ideas in order to understand a cultural context that a person finds themselves living in. The only flaw in the synthetic model as we apply it to conversation that critics have pointed out is, in my opinion, its greatest strength: dialogue.[19]

---

[19] Bevans, *Models of Contextual Theology*, 93.

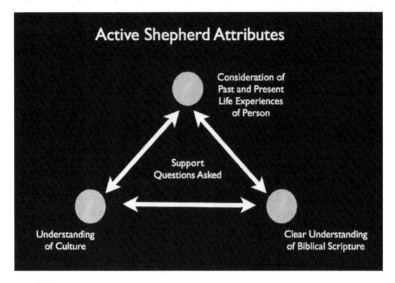

This way of mentoring I call being an *Active Shepherd*.[20] Much like a juggler, we who are mentors have to keep these three ideas in play: conversation, listening, and looking for how the three interrelate. Listening earns us the space to ask *informed questions*. Through time (diachronic) in dialogue, mentees will ask questions back to us. Simply by being a humble and skilled shepherd who cares enough to be with people, a meaningful conversation occurs. We are building our greatest commodity in any relationship: *trust*. We have the privilege, then, to help each other to understand God's perspective on their own past, their present culture, and their future life in considering Christ. When the shepherd sees that the sheep can be led, guided, renewed, and protected, it's then they can also be challenged!

I remember calling up my own youth pastor, Bobby, to ask him how I was to forgive someone in my youth group who was being deliberately spiteful. "How many times am I supposed to

---

[20] Zarns, "Transition Between Teenagers and Young Adults Within the Pentecostal Church of Sweden," 41.

forgive them? Three, four times?" His calm response was, "Seventy times seven."[21] As a mentor, he guided me back to a verse that I knew all too well, and then he left me with the challenge of forgiving. I felt as if I had just been body-slammed with the truth, and deep down, I knew the advice was good and right. I trusted my mentor. One-on-one, I learned from someone who knew my history, my culture, and had a strong understanding of the Bible.

Being an active shepherd is a way of mentoring that has been in place for years. If you are a believer today who began to believe as a child or as a teenager, I'm positive that you can point to either a generational mentor or a leadership mentor who listened to your past and considered your culture and your thoughts about God. He or she gave *you* time and space to ask questions and figure out life. I'd go further to suggest that because this person was an active shepherd to you, you are challenged to be a believer today because of this process.

And I'd bet you became a mentor yourself in some way.

You are a copycat.

Mentoring and Jesus

Some of the most memorable one-on-one meetings found in the Bible are between Jesus and Peter. The failures and triumphs of Peter revolve around his words about who Jesus was. Jesus, knowing Peter's history and his present perspective, asks the entire group of disciples a question. "Who do people say that the Son of Man is?" After they gave their answer, he asked them a more direct question: "Who do you say I am?" A good mentor

---

21 Matt. 18:22.

will give mentees the opportunity to draw their own conclusions. In this moment, after the question was asked, Jesus waited for their inward belief in him to turn into action and come to life. The first to speak up was Peter: "You are the Messiah, the Son of the living God."[22]

Jesus then tells his disciples they "will all run away" in denial of him. "Even if I have to die with you," Peter replied, "I will never deny you!"[23] Wouldn't you know it, but Peter denies knowing Jesus to a crowd on the night before his crucifixion: "I don't know the man!"[24]

After his resurrection, Jesus the Good Shepherd, gives Peter a second chance. "A third time he asked him, "Simon son of John, do you love me?" Peter was hurt that Jesus asked the question a third time. He said, "Lord, you know everything. You know that I love you."[25]

From this we see that Jesus as mentor knew the right answers and could coach even Peter to say things that Peter himself didn't fully understand. Instead, Jesus placed Peter in a process that led to him coming to his own understanding. Jesus led, guided, and renewed Peter, just as God had promised through the psalmist. How could he extend such grace? A shepherd loves his sheep and loves to be with his sheep.

---

[22] Matt. 16:16.

[23] Matt. 26:35.

[24] Matt. 26:74.

[25] John 21:17.

Study Questions:

1. What is the Hebrew word for generations? Which book of the Bible is named after this word?
2. Jesus asks Peter what he believes about Jesus's identity. Why doesn't Jesus just tell him?
3. What is the Latin word for shepherd? Who can be an active shepherd? What is the goal of being an active shepherd in light of Matthew 16:15?

Chapter 5

Setup

I do the work—you watch. I do the work—you help.
You do the work—I help. You do the work—I watch.[1]

Being led by a mentor through a process, we are bound to be different people on the other side. Whether in sports, academics, or on a life-changing spiritual walk, at the end of hard training, we are faster, more skilled, dare I say ... awesome! Think caterpillar to butterfly. When we begin to copycat others, we do so because we want to find a better way to live life. Shepherds/Mentors propel us like a driver to a golf ball Now we are just waiting for a catalyst to drive us down the fairway.

Potential Energy

In 1853, William Rankine introduced the idea of two kinds of energy, *actual* and *potential*, in his paper, "On the General Law of the Transformation of Energy." *Actual energy* is energy of motion, while *potential energy* is energy of position.[2] Picture in your mind a rock boulder sitting atop a hill. There it will sit,

---

[1] Anonymous.

[2] Rankine, *On the General Law of the Transformation of Energy*, 106.

waiting for something or someone to give it a push. The boulder itself holds potential energy that just needs to be released by a catalyst. A mentored process places us into a position to live out a chain reaction of events that will not only lead us to originality, but places us in a position to mentor others. The final four chapters—The Setup, The Drop, Reputation, and Transfer— revolve around unlocking the potential energy inside of each copycat.

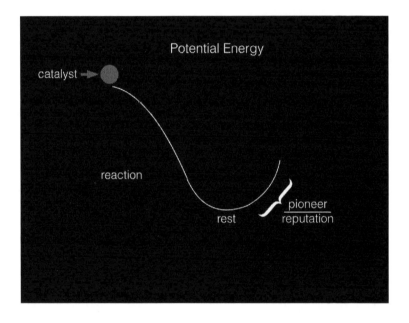

My hope is that we will realize our own potential energy and let God become our catalyst to launch our transition into originality. The Bible holds so many stories about how God positions his people with potential energy and then gives them the inspiring push they need. Whether someone was starting churches or experiencing healing from a hideous skin disease, *transition* is the message of hope we receive when God gets involved in a life.

Catalyst #1 – God's Word

A story passed on for generations, The Bible begins with a transition that is undeniably divine.

> *In the beginning God created the heavens and the earth. Now the earth was formless and empty, darkness was over the surface of the deep, and the Spirit of God was hovering over the waters*[3]

Abruptly, the world transitions from mixed chaos to light. God flexes his power, setting boundaries, creating shape and form. Strassner calls God's actions "forming and filling."[4] These two important actions foreshadow what was about to take place on a macro scale. God spends days one through three on giving form to his new creation, while during days four through six, he fills it with life. What was the catalyst that sparked form and life into being?

Watch this: *"And God said"* is the phrase God spoke at the beginning of each new day. *Mr*[5] is the Hebrew word for "to say," from the root *amar*, "to utter, to address." When God speaks, formations follow. The catalyst of each reaction is *his word*. His yes is a *yes* and his no is a *no*. In other words, what he says, he means. The phrase "chaos to light" is not just a metaphor. It literally is the grand vision for all future reactions between God

---

[3] Gen. 1:1.

[4] Strassner, *Opening Up Genesis*, ch. 1.

[5] Thomas, *New American Standard Hebrew-Aramaic and Greek Dictionaries*, 559.

the Creator and his creation. Later, into the chaos that was Israel would arrive a light that would be the "light of men,"[6] Jesus Christ.

God's self-existence allows him and him alone to say, "I AM who I AM."[7] He reaches out to us out of his desire to "form and fill" creation with humankind[8] and then decides to share with us the responsibility to do the same. In the middle of all of these incredible transitions of light and power, somewhere along the way something went wrong. If there were one force on earth that could rob us of our beloved mentor, it was *sin*.

Adam and Eve - Genesis

After the seven days of creation, God promised the world to Adam and Eve.[9] Seriously, the world! They receive God's blessing, his direction, and his trust. Through God connecting to his creation, some of God's own character shines through them.

In Genesis 2, God gives Adam an important instruction:

> *You may freely eat the fruit of every tree in the garden—except the tree of the knowledge of good and evil. If you eat its fruit, you are sure to die.*[10]

Let's be clear. God did not lead them into a windowless room where the only object was a big, red button with the instructions, "Don't push the button." There was a forest of

---

[6] John 1:4.

[7] Exod. 3:14.

[8] Gen. 1:27.

[9] Gen. 1:28-30.

[10] Gen. 2:16-17.

plenty of other fruit trees from which to grab a bite. One of the first decisions that God allows Adam and Eve to make allows sin to enter the world.

Way to go Adam and Eve. You blew it.

Inheritance of Sin

Imagine a family showing up to the reading of a will.

"And to my first son, I leave to you my raging anger and jealousy. You're welcome!"

Adam and Eve's disobedience becomes the inheritance no one wants. Much like inheriting a set of doilies from Great Aunt Gertrude when we were hoping for her Ferrari. Sin robs us of our potential energy, blocking our dreams of doing anything original for God. Being human, we can't help but be copycats of Adam and Eve. Thank God, there was an alternative inheritance to come!

Pivotal moments in the Bible involve sin and our relationship to it. From poor choices come negative consequences.[11] The conditional Hebrew word *ki*, meaning "because," opens God's judgment as recorded in Genesis on the serpent, woman, and man. There was a decision made and results that followed. For women, childbirth would become painful, accompanying a desire to control their husbands. Their husbands would rule over them.[12] Sin causes disruptions in relationships by pitting people against each other. Men and women would from now on be poised in tension rather than harmony.

---

[11] Gen. 3:6.

[12] Gen. 3:16.

For men, they would become fixated on their work, finding their worth in their labor instead of seeking their worth in God.[13] So if women find their worth in men and men find their worth in work, then Adam and Eve transitioned away from finding their worth in God. Again, sin disrupts relationship. Ever since then, we have been trying to find a way back to how things ought to be.

At this point, nobody wants to copycat Adam and Eve, right? Look at what happens to their kids! The residual effect of their sin spreads to Cain and Abel. God curses two things—the snake and the ground.[14] The inheritance that Cain and Abel receive is a cursed earth, intense pain, and hard labor. Enjoy your doilies, boys. Genesis 4:3-7 tells of how both Cain and Abel brought their offerings to God. Abel gave his best, which pleased God. Cain neither gave his best nor earned God's favor. God warned Cain that his jealousy was becoming a sin. After all, a good shepherd warns his sheep. But Cain allowed his jealousy to grow and murdered his brother.[15] God again uses the Hebrew word *arar* to relate the curse Cain now bore in relationship to the earth. From the fall of humankind[16] to Cain's crime against his brother,[17] there arose a pattern of sin. This pattern becomes God's justification for the flood, which he uses to cleanse the world from unrighteousness.[18]

---

[13] Gen. 3:17-19.

[14] Thomas, *New American Standard Hebrew-Aramaic and Greek Dictionaries*, 779.

[15] Gen. 4:8.

[16] Gen. 3:6.

[17] Gen. 4:8.

[18] Gen. 10.

The "Gift" that Keeps on Giving – Exodus 34: 5-7

By the time of Moses, God decided to shed more light on the characteristics of sin.

The Lord, the Lord, the compassionate and gracious God, slow to anger, abounding in love and faithfulness, maintaining love to thousands, and forgiving wickedness, rebellion and sin. Yet he does not leave the guilty unpunished; he punishes the children and their children for the sin of the parents to the third and fourth generation.[19]

At the same time as God reveals how great his love is, he slips in a statement about the viral and generational nature of sin. The reason that sin gets passed on to our children's children is that the "father" generation had not attempted to correct its own wrongs. It had become an heirloom of God's own people. Sin is disgustingly parasitic, feeding like a lamprey attached to a shark, hanging on until the host dies and then latching onto the next of kin. This is a horrible image, but this is how sin continues to live on.

It's not nice, clean, and tidy, is it? Never fear, true believer.[20] Dillard shares, "While sin spreads and increases, God reveals himself to be long-suffering and patient with his creation,"[21] as a mentor should be. Remember, a good mentor will give second chances. God wanted to restore mankind's potential to follow him as copycats.

---

[19] Exod. 34:6-7.

[20] Lee, *Stan's Soapbox.*

[21] Longman and Dillard, *An Introduction to the Old Testament*, 52.

God restores us by *blessing*. Maybe you have counted yourself out, that there is no hope for you as a mentor, follower, or anything good for that matter. As we look at the transition of sin from one generation to the next, we've also got to pay far more attention to blessing. *Barak*, the Hebrew word for "abundant blessing," is used to describe receiving both tangible and intangible things. There are many types of blessing; the two examples I want to investigate have clear, direct links to our future with God.

You're going to discover that blessing is passed on via both generational mentors and leadership mentors. God's plans for mentorship have a solid, proven, foundation. If sin can be passed through people, so can blessing. This is key to seeing how your own life will be affected. A good boss is a blessing to his or her employees, and you can tell that by how the employees work. A caring teacher is a blessing to his or her students, and you can tell by the way the students study. It's just how things work!

Do Nothing or Do Something

The inheritances of sin and blessing are very different from each other. Plainly said, one is negative and the other positive. The motion required to pass on each inheritance is different as well. It requires *zero* effort to pass sin on to the following generations,[22] because people are born into sin. One can't avoid it. However, blessing involves someone doing something for someone else. Blessing others is a choice. In the Bible, to transfer blessing to others, leaders would lay their hands on people while

---

[22] Rom. 3:23.

praying,[23] they would pour oil on them to physically symbolize God's blessing,[24] and they would speak prayers of blessing over them.[25] The Bible shows us that we must be active in our families and community to pass on and receive blessing. Sitting dormant provokes God to withhold his blessings. The blessings may even disappear, as happened to King Saul because of his disregard for God's command.[26] So how else can God restore us?

Generational Transition

In ancient biblical times, it was lawful that different children received different inheritances from their fathers.[27] The birthright amount bestowed on the eldest son was double the amount fathers gave to their younger son.[28] This way of dividing the estate was an accepted part of their patriarchal culture. The receiver of the birthright also received the right and responsibility of continuing the family name.

The candid story of Jacob and Esau is a strange example of how a birthright can be passed on ... to the second-born son.

---

[23] Mark 10:16.

[24] 1 Sam. 10:1.

[25] Num. 6:24-26.

[26] 1 Sam. 15:27.

[27] Richards, *The Bible Reader's Companion*, Gen. 25:23.

[28] Draper, Brand, and England, eds., *Holman Illustrated Bible Dictionary*.

Jacob & Esau - Genesis 25:5-6

Jacob and Esau were twins born to Isaac and Rebekah. Esau is the first out with Jacob following holding his heel. Even before their birth, Rebekah knew the futures of each child.

> *The Lord said to her, "Two nations are in your womb, and two peoples from within you will be separated; one people will be stronger than the other, and the older will serve the younger."*[29]

Who was the younger? Jacob!

This prophetic message to Rebekah turns the concept of blessing on its head. According to the law of birthright, Esau should receive this gift. One day, it all unfolded. Like a guy, Esau sells his birthright to his younger brother because he was hungry. You might laugh, but this happened more often in families than we think. Archaeological findings from this period describe numerous sales of birthrights in order to get instant gratification. What Jacob was cooking was exactly what Esau wanted.[30] It should have been the best chili in the world for what it cost Esau! Chives and sour cream with that, bro?

The idea of Esau selling his birthright began with tricky Jacob. Esau brushes off any talk of birthright and just redirects the conversation back to his belly. Yet Jacob presses the question, making Esau swear that their agreement would become a binding contract. Good deal for Jacob, bad deal for Esau.

This birthright was loaded with good stuff, as it also contained the right to carry on the *barak* that Abraham had

---

[29] Gen. 25:23.

[30] Gen. 25:29.

received many years earlier.[31] The promise of blessing that God made to Abraham was passed on to Isaac[32] and then to Jacob.[33] Jacob received material wealth, favor, and a growing family. Jacob's potential grew while Esau's decreased. While not favorable for both brothers, a transition occurred.

A word about Jacob: Don't be that guy. The good news is that we don't need to cheat and deceive to get God's blessing into our lives!

Intermission – Elevator Music

Stick with me, friends! We have to do the work to find the backstory of how God transitions blessing between generations before we can unlock how copycats can release their potential. This is part of the process.

Leadership Transition

In the Old Testament times, leadership held a special blessing reserved for prophets and kings. As a birthright was for the firstborn within certain families, leadership would begin to buck the trend and be passed on in a completely different way. It would be passed on across bloodlines, regardless of family background. Both then and now, God considers our heart's posture, not our paternal pedigree. The best-case scenario for leadership shows that it is God who chooses, commissions, and

---

[31] Gen. 12:2.

[32] Gen. 17:19.

[33] Gen. 27:27-29.

encourages each transition.[34] Let's look at two transitions: Joshua succeeding Moses and David succeeding Saul.

Moses to Joshua - Numbers 27:15-23

One of the most revered leaders in the Bible is Moses, who lived a truly epic life. He was sometimes unsure of himself and his role[35] and at other times he was just plain angry.[36] Moses memorably led God's people, all two million of them, out of imperial Egypt in the presence and power of God. While God planned to take Moses into the Promised Land, Moses was stopped cold in his tracks and couldn't enter because of his own disobedience.[37] It was time to find a new leader. What would be the correct process for finding and commissioning a leader of two million people? Here are the exact steps that led to Joshua taking over:

Moses said to the Lord, "May the Lord, the God who gives breath to all living things, appoint someone over this community to go out and come in before them, one who will lead them out and bring them in, so the Lord's people will not be like sheep without a shepherd."

So the Lord said to Moses, "Take Joshua son of Nun, a man in whom is the spirit of leadership, and lay your hand on him. Have him stand before Eleazar the priest and the entire assembly and commission him in their presence. Give him some of your authority so the whole Israelite community will obey him. He is to

---

[34] Cabal, ed., *The Apologetics Study Bible*, Numbers 10.

[35] Exod. 3:11.

[36] Num. 20:11.

[37] Walvoord and Zuck, eds., *Bible Knowledge Commentary*, Num. 27:15-23.

stand before Eleazar the priest, who will obtain decisions for him by inquiring of the Urim before the Lord. At his command he and the entire community of the Israelites will go out, and at his command they will come in."

Moses did as the Lord commanded him. He took Joshua and had him stand before Eleazar the priest and the whole assembly. Then he laid his hands on him and commissioned him, as the Lord instructed through Moses.[38]

Catalyst #2 – The Holy Spirit - Ruach

This chunk of the Bible provides a blueprint for how to choose leadership under the direction and authority of God. First, Moses asks God what to do, which is always a great starting point. God answers Moses's question with *"Joshua son of Nun,"* who had the *"spirit of leadership."* In the original Hebrew, there was no direct mention of leadership, yet the presence of the word *ruach* in this phrase told Hebrew readers more than enough about God's choice.

The word *ruach*, meaning "breath or spirit," was used at decisive moments in biblical history. God's *ruach* was the catalyst for creation. God formed Adam and breathed his *ruach* into him. Since Joshua was living a righteous and obedient life, God recognized him and blessed him with responsibility. In turn, Moses presents Joshua to the priest and to the whole assembly of people and commissions him. Moses shares the leadership responsibilities with Joshua, and later he withdraws completely and gives Joshua full responsibility. Look at the quote at the beginning of this chapter. This is how it's done.

---

[38] Num. 27:15-23.

This passage clearly defines the following seven steps for establishing transition in leadership: (1) asking God to reveal his will, (2) listening for his answer, (3) checking for the presence of God's spirit in the potential leader, (4) presenting the new leader, (5) blessing the leader, (6) sharing power with the current leader, and (7) giving full power to the new leader while withdrawing it from the former leader.

Saul to David - 1 Samuel 16:1-14

The prophet Samuel received a message from God that Saul was to be removed as King mid-reign. Just as God foretold, Saul forfeited God's blessing[39] and Samuel began the search for a replacement king. As commanded by God, Samuel arrives in Bethlehem and finds Eliab, one of Jesse's sons. Samuel was 100 percent sure that Eliab was the guy. God replied,

People look at the outward appearance, but the Lord looks at the heart.[40]

God's plan demands that leaders possess qualities different than those which humans consider important. He says they should find a leader with a true heart.[41] Samuel asks Jesse if he has met all of his sons, to which Jesse responds by sending for David. Samuel then anoints David to become the new King of Israel. The blessing of leadership is passed on.

---

[39] 1 Sam. 15:28.

[40] 1 Sam. 16:7.

[41] Knowles, *The Bible Guide*, 1 Samuel 16.

This is the big one. This is the catalyst that in the beginning of the Bible was going to release the potential that God held within.

God's own spirit is in this blessing—*ruach.*

The spirit of God "came upon David mightily" because of Samuel's blessing. Simultaneously, God's spirit departed from Saul.[42]

Both accounts of Joshua and David involve the choice of God on who will become the successors to Moses and Saul, his spiritual representatives who confirm the new leaders, and the presence of God's spirit in the new leadership. Hard to believe, but in both stories, transitions in leadership happened because of the disobedience on the part of the established leaders. What happens when an established leader doesn't do anything bad but just gets to be old?

Elijah to Elisha - 2 Kings 2:1-15

A truly great example of leadership transition from old to young was that between Elijah and Elisha. Elijah was talking to God, counting himself as the only prophet remaining in Israel when God suddenly names his successor, *"Elisha son of Shaphat from Abel Meholah."*[43] After Elijah throws his cloak on Elisha in an act of sharing his power, Elijah began to walk away.[44]

2 Kings 2 begins with three places where Elijah tested Elisha's loyalty. Bethel, Jericho, and Jordan were all places where God had already done mighty things. *Bethel*, or "house of God,"

---

[42] Dockery, ed., *Holman Bible Handbook*, 1 Sam. 16:14.

[43] 1 Kings 19:14-16.

[44] Walvoord and Zuck, *Bible Knowledge Commentary*, 2 Kings 2.

was where Jacob received Abraham's blessing.[45] Jericho was where God gave an entire enemy fortress to the Israelites as a consequence of Joshua's obedience.[46] The Jordan was the river the Israelites had crossed on dry land between walls of water to enter the Promised Land.[47] Elijah tells Elisha to stay and not follow him before departing each location. Three times Elisha refuses and follows loyally, saying,

As surely as the Lord lives and as you live, I will not leave you.

Kind of a Peter-esque moment. Finally, they arrive at the Jordan River, and Elijah hits the river with his cloak. Just the two of them walk across the water, leaving behind the fifty other tag-a-long prophets following them.[48] The prophetic training schools of that day operated under mentor-disciple relationships. In some cases, the depth of a father-son relationship could grow into that between a disciple and his mentor.[49] Elisha's reason to be close to Elijah may have been his hope for the inheritance of God's spirit on his own life.[50] In fact, Walvoord says that most young people in those times did not want to be away from a dying parent's side for fear of missing a blessing.[51]

This is Elisha's moment. Elisha asks,

---

[45] Gen. 28:19.

[46] Josh. 6:2-5.

[47] Josh. 3:14-17.

[48] 2 Kings 2:7.

[49] Freeman, *The New Manners and Customs of the Bible*, 2 Kings 2.

[50] Richards, *The Bible Reader's Companion*, 2 Kings 2.

[51] Walvoord and Zuck, eds., *Bible Knowledge Commentary*.

"Let me inherit a double portion of your spirit."

Elijah replies,

"You have asked a difficult thing, yet if you see me when I am taken from you, it will be yours—otherwise, it will not."

Elisha watches his master rise to heaven on a fiery chariot, the most hard-rock exit of all time! Instantly, Elisha gets what he wanted. Elisha, hurt by Elijah's departure, cries out, "Father!" Their prophetic relationship had grown to be like that of father and son.[52]

This transition of leadership from Elijah to Elisha was a ten-year discipleship process. We also see the transition from father to son as a patriarchal blessing. In this way, Elisha receives the *birthright* from his *father*, Elijah. God named the successor, the prophet confirmed him, and the spirit of God—*ruach*—began to embody the works of the new leader as his mentor leaves him in charge.

Wrap-up

Each transition in leadership brings attention (glory) to God. Remember, he chooses his leaders. God wanted to realign his creation to a position where he could bless future generations of leaders and heirs.[53]

Two catalysts had ignited the *potential energy* in their successors. The first catalyst was the Word of God, which set the entire earth into *active energy*. Second, the presence of God's

---

[52] Freeman, *The New Manners and Customs of the Bible.*

[53] Gen. 12:1-3.

spirit on earth took a central role in the leadership transitions. There is a third catalyst that we'll dedicate the next chapter to: Jesus Christ.

A New Jacket

At the core of a transition, a leader gives someone else the opportunity and right to lead. Mentors have an enormous role in this, as does the process of raising up another leader to take their place. When you have submitted to a process and to a mentor, you are positioned with potential energy to make right choices and to do something that no one has done before.

My friend and boss, Tim, told me a story that an English friend once told him. It was about the school uniforms that English schoolboys once wore. Each student would be sent to public school with a new jacket for that year. It was a suit coat jacket, with some buttons as you might imagine running down one side. In the autumn, the cuffs of the sleeves came down to about the middle of their hands. As time went by and the jacket became well-worn, the student began to realize that the jacket had not gotten smaller, but that he had grown into the jacket. By the time of summer recess, the tattered cuffs would stop at the wrists. Come autumn, as you might have guessed, he got a new jacket.

Maybe you have gone through a process; you've had mentors, you're waiting on God, and nothing is happening. It could be that you are still trying to hang on to the old jacket, so to speak, of things you used to do. A habit, a way of thinking, friends. You might still be keeping the old ways of life close by you.

Take on the blessing that God is promising you through mentorship via his Spirit working in your heart. What you have to do is let go of your old jacket, your old self. Now I challenge you as Tim did me:

Put on the new jacket. It's a new season. Grow into it.

Study Questions:

1. What is the difference between actual and potential energy?
2. David and Saul were both Kings of Israel at different times. What was transferred from Saul to David to signal the change in leadership?
3. What response does Elijah give to Elisha when he asked for a double portion of the spirit? Why is Elisha allowed to see Elijah depart?

Chapter 6

Spark

You should consider that Imitation is the most acceptable part of Worship, and that the Gods had much rather Mankind should Resemble, than Flatter them. That Operation is the right Proof of Nature; That Trees are distinguished by their Fruit.[1]

A world record, 272,297 dominos toppled, one after another on a summer afternoon in Büdingen, Germany, was set on July 12, 2013.[2] Twelve builders set aside eight days to meticulously set up each tile, measuring the space between each so that the timing and chain reaction would work flawlessly. They documented the nearly ten minutes it took the dominoes to fall, inviting the media and a live audience to witness the event. After painstakingly installing the aerial tricks, crazy designs, and curving trails, the entire reaction began with the fall of a single domino. With cameras rolling, this one domino was the catalyst, releasing the potential energy of the entire mosaic!

---

[1] Aurelius et al., *Emperor Marcus Antoninus*, 339.

[2] Subramanian, "272,297 Dominoes Fall for New World Record," para. 1.

Jesus Christ was and is the catalyst to the multicultural mosaic of people around the world! The New Testament begins,

This is the genealogy of Jesus the Messiah the son of David, the son of Abraham.[3]

I know it's just what you were hoping for—reading through someone's Ancestry.com entry. Don't worry, this is far, far more interesting than finding out that your third cousin twice removed used to be a roadie for Fleetwood Mac.

Tracing the generations of blessing from Abraham to Jesus Christ was a way of using the Hebrew tradition of respect for the lineage of families and tribes to prove the legitimacy of Jesus as the Messiah.[4] The Greek of Matthew 1:1 mirrors quite closely the Hebrew of Genesis 5:1:

This is the written account of Adam's family line.

The blessing from long ago was about to resurface. The transition of God's blessing from *toledot* to *toledot* was just getting warmed up. It takes a new direction with Jesus Christ, and God's blessing is passed on to all humankind. Jesus made a way for us to be his copycats.

---

[3] Matt. 1:1.

[4] Matt. 1:6; Jer. 23:5-6.

Early in John 1, Jesus is described as,

He who was with God in the beginning.

Not only did Jesus exist before time began, but from the outset, Jesus is described as One who held life within him.[5] The fullness of life is found in him, in a self-existent way as it was in the beginning with God the Father. John describes that life as light that overcomes the darkness.

Light (*phōs* in the Greek), simply put, makes things visible. How close we stand in relationship to a light source determines how much we see with it. The stars in the night sky may appear as tiny, flickering lights against the blackness of space. But when we shift our perspective and get up close and personal with the sun, for example, our perspective of the light it radiates is totally different!

Staring up at the noontime sun on a real scorcher of a day, it's nearly impossible to escape the light. Because of its northern latitude, summertime in Stockholm, Sweden, meant that we had to seal up the bedroom windows because the sun shone twenty hours a day! One definition of light, the wave-particle theory, holds that light is made up of small particles that follow a wave-shaped pattern traveling in a certain direction.[6] The wave-shaped pattern gives light the ability to *bend*. So even if a person hides behind a corner to try to escape direct sunlight, the light will bend and find him or her. Darkness can't overcome light when

---

[5] Thomas, *New American Standard Hebrew-Aramaic and Greek Dictionaries.*

[6] Wave-particle theory, widely accepted by research scientists.

we keep the light close to us! The closer we are to the light, the more visible life becomes. That is how life becomes when we dare to live closely to the light of Jesus. Everything is visible and out in the open.

Jesus and Cousin John – John 1:6

About two hundred years before Jesus was born, a group of Jews called the Essenes went to live in the wilderness at Qumran. This strict community believed that someone special would be coming out of the wilderness.

A voice of one calling in the desert, "Prepare the way for the Lord, make straight paths for Him."[7]

Like people waiting for fireworks on the Fourth of July, the Essenes set up their lawn chairs and waited.

The *paths* mentioned in the same verse may not have been literal roadways. Isaiah wrote about creating pathways into and out of our hearts! The Essene community wanted to get their hearts ready for the coming of the Lord by turning from their old sinful ways of living. If they needed to be forgiven, they would do whatever they could to make things right with others. This was their way of becoming whole again with God. When someone wanted to become a part of the community, they would be immersed (or baptized) in water to signify the death and burial of their old life and the birth of their new life.[8]

John the Baptist arrives from the wilderness, wearing the same trendy Prophet garb that Elijah had worn: a camel's hair

[7] Isa. 40:3.

[8] 2 Cor. 5:17.

tunic and a leather belt.⁹ Keeping his diet rich in protein and sugar, he ate locusts dipped in honey. John may or may not have been a member of the Essene community. What we do know is that his message was similar to how the Essenes lived. His and their message was, "Repent—that is, turn around and go in the opposite direction of sin—for the Kingdom of Heaven is near!"¹⁰

John taught people they needed to be baptized as a way of showing that they had chosen to live a new and God-centered life. The more that people saw God's light in John, the more people drew near to God. Clarity was happening in their lives, and this change was attractive.

But John makes it crystal clear that he was paving the way for One even greater than himself:

*He cried out, saying, "This is the one I spoke about when I said, 'He who comes after me has surpassed me because he was before me.'"*¹¹

If that didn't sound modest enough, John also declared:

*"I baptize you with water for repentance. But after me comes one who is more powerful than I, whose sandals I am not worthy to carry. He will baptize you with the Holy Spirit and fire."*¹²

Fire. John could have said any word, but God directed him to say *fire*. John was light, but he was not THE light. The most

---

⁹ 2 Kings 1:8.

¹⁰ Matt. 3:2.

¹¹ John 1:8, 15.

¹² Matt. 3:11.

honorable attribute of John is that he knew his place. He was second, while Christ would be first.

Jesus became the catalyst who would light up the whole world, while John was working as hard as he could to awaken one part of that world.

John understood that in order for Jesus to gain the attention of all, his own light needed to diminish so that Jesus's light could increase.[13] Sometimes that's the way it works in leadership. It may be that someone came to pioneer a new work, but someone else entirely shows up to complete the job. Being close to God's light will reveal to us our place and our role. We could learn a lot by copycatting John's humility.

Baptizo

> *Then Jesus came from Galilee to the Jordan to be baptized by John. But John tried to deter him, saying, "I need to be baptized by you, and do you come to me?"*
>
> *Jesus replied, "Let it be so now; it is proper for us to do this to fulfill all righteousness." Then John consented.*

John was greatly respected by people who came to him from both near and far to be water-baptized.[14] Yet John was expecting that Jesus should baptize him, since he was a lesser man of God than Jesus. Jesus insisted however that John baptize him! The importance of this is that Jesus came to fulfill a prophecy spoken

---

[13] John 3:30.

[14] Willard, *The Divine Conspiracy*, 17.

hundreds of years earlier.[15] He had come to light up the whole world, to start something global.

> *As soon as Jesus was baptized, he went up out of the water. At that moment heaven was opened, and he saw the Spirit of God descending like a dove and alighting on him. And a voice from heaven said, "This is my Son, whom I love; With him I am well pleased."*[16]

God the Father was and is justifiably proud of his Son. Jesus was showing us how to live, calling us to copycat him.

Equipping the Disciples and the 72

Like a good, *active shepherd*, Jesus spent a lot of time with his flock, the disciples. They ate together, played backgammon, went ox-tipping at night ... Really, he was devoted to showing them what a changed world could look like because of God's light! In Luke 8, Jesus told inspiring parables, he calmed a storm with a command, healed a man who was demon-possessed, and brought a small girl back to life. If we only had one chapter of the Bible that told us about Jesus, this would be a good one!

I hope you remember potential energy. I'm sure you do. I've typed it enough times. This part of the story is where Jesus becomes the catalyst to his disciples, setting their lives into motion!

In Luke 9:1-2, Jesus transitions the disciples from being stationary spectators to becoming workers themselves. Luke tells us that he *"gave them power and authority ..."* To do what? To do

---

[15] Isa. 42:1.

[16] Matt. 3:13–17.

exactly what he just did! *"... to drive out demons and to cure diseases, and he sent them out proclaiming the kingdom of God, and to heal the sick."* A leadership mentor, proactive in directing his followers, can help them develop their potential energy into *active energy.* Whether it is through God's word, the Holy Spirit, or Jesus himself, God is ready to be our catalyst. Inseparable, each part of the Triune God shepherds us into his kingdom.

Power Shared

Displaying his power at the creation of the world, God's expression of his love for us only increased with the passage of time.[17] My friends, Anita and John Koeshall, have written extensively about how God shared his power with us through Jesus Christ.[18]

> *Being in very nature God, [he] did not consider equality with God something to be grasped, but made himself nothing, taking the very nature of a servant, being made in human likeness.*[19]

This servant was willing to create the way for us to follow in his footsteps. He didn't have to die, but he chose to give his life —which is even greater proof of his humility! How could we even hope to copycat Jesus's humility? We are smelly, loud sheep, after all! We are dormant, stationary. Sometimes we have no desire outside of pleasing ourselves. To be more like Jesus, we

---

[17] Zarns, *The Soundtrack of Your Life*, loc. 719.

[18] Koeshall, "Redeemed Power in Action: A Prerequisite for a Generous Ecclesiology," 2011.

[19] Phil. 2:6-8.

must be transformed so deeply within ourselves that the very attention and direction of our souls has been altered.

> *Consequently, just as one trespass resulted in condemnation for all people, so also one righteous act resulted in justification and life for all people. For just as through the disobedience of the one man the many were made sinners, so also through the obedience of the one man the many will be made righteous.*[20]

Jesus came to earth to free humankind from the chaos of sin, shedding new light, and sharing his life, one that has no end. Just as all people are born in sin, Jesus calls us out into his light and forgiveness.[21]

Jesus makes it possible for all people to transition into blessing. We are too weak to even be able to believe that in our own strength. It is only through the power of the Holy Spirit, who bonds with our spirit, that we can hear God's word about Jesus Christ … and believe it to be true.[22] All three catalysts have their place in causing God's kingdom to flourish in our hearts. Where Jesus is King, there is his kingdom.

Mission - Matthew 28:18-20

Just before ascending into heaven, Jesus gave his followers a compelling command:

> *Then Jesus came to them and said, "All authority in heaven and on earth has been given to me. Therefore go and make disciples of all nations, baptizing them in the name of the Father and of the*

---

[20] Ladd, *A Theology of the New Testament*, Rom. 5:18-19.

[21] Rom. 3:23.

[22] Koeshall, "Redeemed Power in Action: A Prerequisite for a Generous Theology," 7.

*Son and of the Holy Spirit, and teaching them to obey everything
I have commanded you. And surely I am with you always, to the
very end of the age."*

In the presence of more than seven hundred people, Jesus
used the Aramaic equivalent of the Greek word *exousia*, which
means "power to act,"[23] to show the extent of his divine power,
the power with which he equips all who believe in him.[24] Next,
he told them and us what he wanted the church to do—to make,
baptize, and teach disciples.[25] And through these three actions to
reach all nations with the Gospel.[26]

Making disciples means copying the ways of Jesus himself,
learning through a mentored process of discipline.

Baptizing new disciples shows that they have publicly turned
toward God "in the name of the Father, the Son, and the Holy
Spirit."[27] Baptism carries with it the sweet composure[28] of
identifying new believers with Jesus Christ.[29] At each baptism in
the Lutheran church I grew up in, we spoke this verse aloud,

*... let your light shine before others, that they may see your good
deeds and glorify your Father in heaven.*[30]

---

[23] Thomas, *New American Standard Hebrew-Aramaic and Greek Dictionaries*, 1849.

[24] Walvoord and Zuck, *Bible Knowledge Commentary*, Matt 28:18-20.

[25] Bosch, *Transforming Mission*, 65.

[26] Ladd, *A Theology of the New Testament*, 226.

[27] Stronstad, *Full Life Bible Commentary to the New Testament*, 252.

[28] Morris, *The Epistle to the Romans*, 248.

[29] Rom. 6:3.

[30] Matt. 5:16.

Such a beautiful, full verse. After that, the people of the congregation would vow to teach each child what Jesus had commanded, passing on the same challenge that Jesus shared so long ago. On every person who becomes a disciple, is baptized, and is being taught all about Jesus, God's light shines![31]

Jesus then took a final look at the crowd, shouted, "Peace, I'm outta here!" Of course, I'm kidding. For his exit, he levitated out of view. Why did he levitate?

Because he could. After all, Jesus if God.

Redefining an Inclusive Family

Jesus paid the price for our wrongdoing, yes, but he didn't die so we'd become slaves to God. He had a different plan altogether. Because of his willing sacrifice,[32] Jesus fulfilled the law as set forth by God through Moses,[33] offered salvation to the world, and set up a way for anyone to become part of the family of God.[34] He wanted us to become God's *spiritual* children by imparting to us his Spirit.[35]

Did you get that?

All the Bible passages we read in the last chapter about generations, bloodlines, and receiving God's blessing just became open to all!

I repeat, becoming a believer is open to everyone!

---

[31] Matt. 28:20.

[32] Matt. 26:39, John 10:18.

[33] Matt. 5:17-20.

[34] John 3:16.

[35] Thomas, *New American Standard Hebrew–Aramaic and Greek Dictionaries*, 5043.

The Holy Spirit was involved in the creation, in leadership transitions, and even in Jesus's conception,[36] now he is the formative power of faith too!

Huiothesia is a compound Greek word meaning "adoption." It is made up of the two Greek words, *huios* (son) and *tithemi* (committed). Romans 8:15-17 shows that we have opportunity to be adopted through the Holy Spirit and so become "co-heirs" with Christ. We're not just inheriting doilies, y'all! This was originally reserved for the nation of Israel,[37] but now it is open to all. Please forgive the overuse of exclamation marks. I am excited.

The Drop and Jesus

Let's recap the last two chapters. God, the Creator of all, began the idea of transition. Humankind inherited the care of the earth from God. Disobedience in the Garden of Eden led instead to an inheritance of sin, which was passed on to all people. This curse became the source of all the pain and brokenness the world has known since then.

The inheritance of blessing passes from parent to child. In other types of inheritance, leaders would hand over spiritual leadership to capable people whom God specifically qualifies for service.

A clean heart is the qualification for receiving God's blessing of his Holy Spirit in both leadership and inheritance!

Through Jesus, God offers the forgiveness of sins to all people who accept by faith his Son's sacrifice on the cross. As

---

[36] Matt. 1:20.

[37] Nanos, *The Mystery of Romans: The Jewish Context of Paul's Letter*, 112.

"co-heirs" with Jesus in respect to God the Father, we have the power to make new disciples and to baptize and teach them.

What adventure is waiting for us right now? Are we ready to be pushed out of our comfort zones?

Study Questions:

1. What metaphor does John use to describe Jesus Christ?
2. Why did Jesus choose to come into the world the way he did? How does this challenge the way you view your understanding of power?
3. The inheritance of blessing started out as being transferred from the Father to the Son. Has Jesus compelled you to the point of becoming a follower?

Chapter 7

Reputation

Reputation is what men and women think of us; character is what God and the angels know of us.[1]

Every time we explore scientific theory, we discover more of who we are as copycats. We've looked at Batesian-Müllerian mimicry in butterflies, Newton's First Law of motion, photo electricity, Xerox, various university research studies, potential energy, and the wave-particle theory of light. That's a lot of science!

With the billions of dollars spent on research each year, our most solid theories are our best attempts at defining how the world already works. Our science is for us.

We've discovered gravity, crossbred plants to help combat world hunger, battled bacteria with antibiotics, and curbed viral outbreaks with vaccines. Everything we have made was with building blocks that had been lying around for years. Whether it be building the world's tallest skyscraper or forming a new molecule out of photons,[2] the base material was *already present*. It had already been created. It seems that the pinnacle of our

---

[1] Attributed to Thomas Paine (1737-1809).

[2] Firstenberg, "Attractive Photons in a Quantum Nonlinear Medium," para. 1.

existence is to learn from material and ideas we have already discovered and then to find out how we relate to them.

The Problem

Despite our best efforts in science and knowledge, we can't seem to come up with something out of nothing. We are destined to copycat, be it learning from nature or from each other. Honestly, it's kind of a downer and a relief at the same time. If we could create something out of nothing, *ex nihilo*, it would be so sweet. Dark chocolate and cappuccinos at the snap of my fingers! At the same time, we must understand our limitations. I'll venture a guess. Boundaries were set in place because it's in our nature to push our discoveries to unhealthy levels.

Theories have been around for thousands of years regarding the existence of atomic particles. J. J. Thompson, who would earn the Nobel Prize for physics in 1906 for his work, first discovered proof of the electron in 1897.[3] The core of an atom is made up of positrons and neutrons, while the electrons orbit around the nucleus. Keep this in mind: Thompson didn't create the electron, he only discovered it.

Following Thompson's research, the early 1900s became a melting pot of experimental work with nuclear physics. Subsequently, the first studies on atomic theory were published shortly thereafter. Thompson found the existence of electrons, but scientist and fellow Nobel laureate Otto Hahn was interested in how neutrons could be released from the atomic core itself. Fueled by his curiosity, Hahn discovered atomic fission, a

---

[3] Thompson, "Carriers of Negative Electricity," 146.

process that not only uncouples a few neutrons, but releases incredible amounts of energy at the same time. This technology became the basis for an intense chain reaction of fission, the core technology of the atomic bomb. Albert Einstein wrote a letter to US President Franklin Delano Roosevelt, describing the capabilities of the atomic bomb as a stealth weapon:

> *A single bomb of this type, carried by boat and exploded in a port, might very well destroy the whole port together with some of the surrounding territory.*[4]

After two atomic bombs claimed 250,000 Japanese lives in 1945, many people realized that we had pushed the envelope too far in the name of both science and our hope for world peace.

In the interest of results, a deadly action occurred, and sadly, was copied. Loved ones were lost and families were decimated in the blink of an eye. The second atomic bomb aided in ending WWII, but at a horrific cost.

This idea of a chain reaction can be redeemed, however. Energy is released because of a catalyst, that then produces hundreds of thousands of other reactions of energy through bonds of relationship.

We know God can be our catalyst. So what's next?

The Chain Reaction - The Downward Slope

We are meant to relate to God and to each other, not to develop and perfect how to destroy each other. He set up the playground of the world so that life together could be *good*, the word he uses to describe his reaction to each stage of his

---

[4] Einstein, "Letter from Albert Einstein to President Franklin Delano Roosevelt," para. 3.

creation. God himself is the catalyst who can get our lives rolling again. You may have been stationary, sitting in the same spot for a very long time. God's Spirit is the catalyst who will ignite your soul and set off a chain reaction of incredible life events.

One of the by-products of a relationship with God is true creativity. This spark is evident in every medium of creation.[5] Have you ever lived around musicians, students, or artists? If you have spent any time around them, you will experience music, learn something new, and be exposed to all sorts of artistic expressions. After living in a creative environment, we can begin to express ourselves much as they do. When we're in *close* proximity to another, we subconsciously become like him or her in some small way. You become their copycat.

If you are chasing after originality, why wouldn't you want to be close to God the Creator of all, and the Author of creativity itself? Furthermore, what could happen through you as a result of your relationship with him? Remember the idea of a chain reaction!

Peter's Reaction - Acts 2

Remember Peter? He fearfully hid himself when asked if he claimed Jesus as his friend. Of course, Jesus as his mentor gave him a second chance. By this point of his life, Peter had learned much about God's character by experiencing his forgiveness. Jesus instructed his disciples to wait for inspiration, to wait for *the helper*,[6] the catalyst. While they waited, the following transpired.

---

[5] Qualls, "Theology Belongs to the Artists as Much As It Does the Apologists," 14.

[6] Acts 1:8.

When the day of Pentecost came, they were all together in one place. Suddenly a sound like the blowing of a violent wind came from heaven and filled the whole house where they were sitting. They saw what seemed to be tongues of fire that separated and came to rest on each of them. All of them were filled with the Holy Spirit and began to speak in other tongues as the Spirit enabled them.[7]

Once they experienced this awesome event, the stubborn man we once knew as Peter took his place as a bold[8] and spiritually insightful leader of the disciples. God's Spirit had transformed him. He was about to flex his leadership by doing something that he had done before, yet now in the grip of a completely different Spirit about him.

He spoke up.

He spoke up in front of people from all different cultures and contexts and delivered an unbending message:

Therefore let all Israel be assured of this:

God has made this Jesus, whom you crucified, both Lord and Messiah.

When the people heard this, they were cut to the heart and said to Peter and the other apostles,

"Brothers, what shall we do?"

Peter replied, "Repent and be baptized, every one of you, in the name of Jesus Christ for the forgiveness of your sins. And you will receive the gift of the Holy Spirit. The promise is for you and your

---

[7] Acts 2:1-4.

[8] Utley, *Luke the Historian*, Acts 2:14.

> *children and for all who are far off—for all whom the Lord our*
> *God will call."*[9]

God loves to use the gifting we developed as copycats in new ways that surprise our friends, family, and communities … and bring attention to him through it all.

The Connection

This is what we've been searching for. Two people, God and Peter, who were disconnected by sin were now connected in power, and so were able to do together something entirely original. This is what God can do with a person's life. The Holy Spirit became the catalyst to release Peter's potential energy. Because Peter lived in close proximity to Jesus, he had formed a relationship with God himself, and so helped to create a relationship between God and every single person who was listening to him. All nations could have the same relationship with God, the original Author, the inexhaustible source. Trusting in any other source pales in comparison to the love, the care, and the creative power that flows from the Holy Spirit. This same Spirit that was active in the beginning of time is present today.

This is the reaction that seems ungraspable, yet is attainable; it's unseen, yet entirely present … and it is only found in a personal relationship with God. One thing we are able to do that is entirely original is to relate one person to another, to connect ourselves to God, and to be powered by God's Spirit. When we inhabit a transformed and creative life, we cannot help but be

---

[9] Acts 2:36-39.

like Peter and do things that we had never had the desire nor the bravery to do before.

Create – the Upward Climb

The only being who can exist alone without needing a single relationship with any person or thing is God himself. After all, God said, *I AM*.[10] With the help of a mentor, God as our catalyst can set us into motion. The trajectory of our lives is something like rolling down a hill, resting at the bottom, and then rolling up the other side. On the way down we react, but on the way we break into uncharted territory.

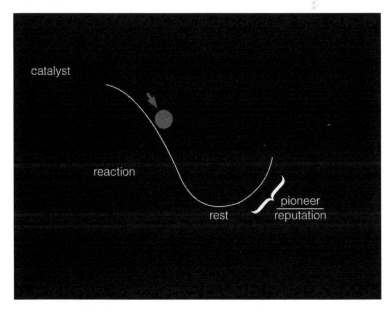

God has given us a gift: the ability to relate two separate objects to each other in order to create something entirely original. Consider the genius of Thomas Edison.

---

[10] Exod. 3:14.

Edison

As a boy, Edison sold newspapers near a railway junction in Detroit. Seeing a boy playing on the tracks, he dropped his papers and pulled the child to safety just in time from an oncoming train. Little did he know that this boy's father was the railway station agent.[11] Edison was offered an internship on the spot in return for his act of courage. He was trained, mentored, and began his work as a railway telegraph operator, relaying and sending messages. This was a precursor to how he would direct and send electric currents through his future inventions.

In his later years, after a thousand failed attempts, his light bulb glowed into life! His first light bulb had a very short life span, yet he soon improved previous designs using a carbon filament that would burn much longer. He continued inventing and developing, producing a telegraph machine, the stock ticker, the phonograph, and the single-unit battery, which would one day power our beloved mobile phones! With each idea and each new relationship of metal and glass, his reputation kept growing and growing. I love inventions, though I'm still waiting for my Hoverboard!

Known

You may one day invent something useful to change the world for the better as Edison did. His reputation is one of a great businessman and creator.

I would argue that what is of even greater worth are those ideas that connect people together. Through those relationships

---

[11] Dyer and Martin, *Edison*, loc. 602.

we share life. Further, when God becomes our catalyst, originality flows from him and into and through us. Transition after transition, God passed on his blessings through every generation beginning with Abraham and reaching its pinnacle with Jesus.

> *I will make you into a great nation,*
> *and I will bless you;*
> *I will make your name great,*
> *and you will be a blessing.*[12]

N.T. Wright reflects on this blessing:

> *Abraham and his descendants are somehow to be the means of*
> *God putting things to rights, the spearhead of God's rescue*
> *operation.*[13]

We've read of the humility of Jesus Christ and his desire to reconnect God with his creation. Jesus created a new and better way for us to live! He also came to increase the reputation of God so that all might trust him. He raised the dead to life, and he freed the demon-possessed. He restored people emotionally and physically. He became the light in their darkness. He offered living water to the thirsty and the bread of life to the hungry.

Today, when a broken heart is connected to God, it is healed. When a husband and wife are planning to divorce, God can heal their broken marriage. God continually creates new life by connecting individual people to himself and to each other. Although Edison had some incredible inventions, Jesus achieved infinitely more: He created a renewable chain of relationships

---

[12] Gen. 12:2.

[13] Wright, *Simply Christian*, loc. 1088.

that today form his church—so that his disciples will go forth and make other disciples!

Reputation and Jesus

I guarantee that if you are looking for a new *anything*, you will certainly find it in a relationship with God as you submit to his process, his mentorship, and allow him to become the catalyst of your life.

We've set you up to let God give you the push you need to get going in your life with him. When you trust him, a new reputation begins. What do you want people to say about you? Would people recognize you as someone who has connected others to God?

Study Questions:

1. In what ways did the message of Peter in Acts 2 resemble a chain reaction?
2. What moments of creativity have you seen in your life, no matter how small you might consider them to be?
3. What do you hope you will be remembered for?

Chapter 8

Transfer

To make disciples, you have to be a disciple.[1]

At age eighteen, I found myself cruising down the road alongside my friend Travis on my 1982 Yamaha motorcycle. It was an incredible feeling. Ahead lay only opportunity, possibility, and freedom!

Where did I think I would be now in my life? Cruising down the road on a Harley-Davidson Heritage Softail, that's where! Easy-riding chrome. Nothing but my gal, the open road, and me. That's exactly where I thought I would be. Now approaching age forty, the arc of my life hasn't taken me anywhere near what I had expected.

Generative vs. Self-Absorption

In all sincerity, if there were a telltale sign that I would be going through a midlife crisis, one can only speculate. Erik Erikson, a brilliant developmental psychologist, marked eight different stages to our development as humans. Erikson's seventh

---

[1] Sigfrids, "DBS," 2014.

stage, *generativity vs. self-absorption*,[2] posits the idea of a midlife crisis and points to a critical moment that will happen in a person's life. Generativity, being the positive side of the two concepts, means that a person would care for others, passing his or her experience and hope on to the next generation of copycats. Generative people invite creativity and productive behavior. In short, they like doing things for others.

Self-absorption, on the other hand, means that he or she *does not care to care* about others, seeking instead a life lived in comfort to one's self. Unless a person moves into the stage of generativity, stagnation can take place by placing the focus solely on self-preservation until life ends.[3] Citizen Kane had style, but he was alone with lost relationships, laden with regret.

Erikson wrote that there's a possibility of the self-absorbed person regressing to an earlier conflict in life, the lessons of which went unlearned. For example, if you didn't learn how to share your toys in the toddler stage, this problem could resurface when you are sixty years old.

What can we learn from generativity vs. self-absorption? Whatever we spend our time on building our reputation will decide what we are going to pass on to the next generation. The generative will share, while the self-absorbed won't. The generative will mentor; the self-absorbed will not.

As generative mentors, we can support the coming generation through their growth process by helping them to find God as their catalyst, and then watch them cause a chain reaction of events in their own lives that will become their

---

[2] Erikson and Erikson, *The Life Cycle Completed*, loc. 818.

[3] Collins, *Christian Counseling*, 200.

reputation. It's not just for the sake of their reputation, however. If we support them, then a part of our reputation grows as well.

The kind of reputation we are building has a lot to do with the nature of our catalyst in those formative years.

Paul writes about the differences in the ways that adults speak, think, and reason, compared to those of a child:

When I was a child, I spoke like a child, I thought like a child, I reasoned like a child. When I became a man, I gave up childish ways.

When I became a man, I gave up my childish ways.[4]

There will be no midlife crisis when we know what we live for. When a person chooses to be giving and caring, they will mature. What does Paul say keeps us like a child? It is the conscious decision not to grow!

Who can help us to make the right choices? The Holy Spirit works in us, helping us copycat the same humility and selflessness of Jesus as expressed in Philippians 2. If there is no Holy Spirit, no Christlike influence, no hearing God's word, then it's much more probable that people who have not heard the Gospel will be on the self-absorption side of Erikson's theory.

Picture this: A young adult realizes the responsibility that comes with being an adult, but then chooses to stay as a child. That person will become an adult in terms of physical age, but will remain inwardly an undeveloped child.[5] In essence, if this same person were never mentored to share or give, the grown

---

[4] 1 Cor. 13:11.

[5] Prime, *Opening Up 1 Corinthians*, 1 Cor. 13:11.

child won't give either, nor will their children, nor their children's children.

A Kingdom Near, A Kingdom Advanced

> *Love never ends. As for prophecies, they will pass away; as for tongues, they will cease; as for knowledge, it will pass away. For we know in part and we prophesy in part, but when the perfect comes, the partial will pass away.*

> *When I was a child, I spoke like a child, I thought like a child, I reasoned like a child. When I became a man, I gave up childish ways.*

> *For now we see in a mirror dimly, but then face to face. Now I know in part; then I shall know fully, even as I have been fully known. So now faith, hope, and love abide, these three; but the greatest of these is love.[6]*

This passage is often read at weddings since it is about God's love. Yet it's surrounded by verses that speak to *growing up*. Paul speaks of knowing a little, then knowing a lot; and a dimly lit mirror and broad daylight. So it is with a married couple. Before they married they were getting to know each other, and afterwards and for years to come they will come to learn about and understand each other on a deeper level. God's love becomes the superglue that holds a marriage together and helps them avoid their midlife crisis. God is the superglue that bonds people together in heart, soul, mind, and faith.

Although it is a nice metaphor to use in a ceremony, this whole passage illustrates how it will be to experience heaven for the first time. Further, in order to foreshadow and give us a taste

---

[6] 1 Cor. 13:8-13.

of being with God in his kingdom, heaven, we have been given an opportunity to experience that same kingdom here on earth, already near to us.

John the Baptist and Jesus shared a message,

Repent [turn around], for the kingdom of heaven has come near.[7]

Matthew in his Gospel refers to the K*ingdom of Heaven*, while Mark, Luke, and John in their Gospels call it the *Kingdom of God*. Either way, Jesus consistently taught in parables about the kingdom. He said the Kingdom of God was like:

- A mustard seed that grew into a strong tree[8]
- A pearl that a man sold everything to gain[9]
- A seed thrown onto a field[10]
- A net that caught all sorts of fish[11]

Each one of these parables is about seemingly powerless objects that have great potential energy. The people had seen Jesus perform many miracles right before their eyes. His hope was that the parables might reach areas of unbelief in their hearts that the miracles had not penetrated.[12]

Here are two simple thoughts about the Kingdom of God as expressed in the Bible.

---

[7] Matt. 3:2.

[8] Matt. 13: 18-23.

[9] Matt. 13:31-32.

[10] Matt. 13:44.

[11] Matt. 13: 47-50.

[12] Luke 8:10.

First, on an internal level, wherever we allow God to establish his reign in our hearts through faith, there we will find the Holy Spirit transforming our character. We are to bear the likeness, be copycats of Jesus Christ, with the Holy Spirit here to help us. When we acknowledge the Holy Spirit's presence within us, God can and will actually change us in due course. Change cannot be avoided! He gives us a new process, a new mentor, and as a result, a new reputation in the Kingdom of God! When he recalibrates our compasses, we get set to head in the right direction!

Second, externally, the kingdom is found *near* to wherever God is proclaimed King.[13] Just as when Jesus sent out first the twelve disciples and then the seventy-two, the kingdom came near to each household they visited, regardless of whether they were made welcome or not. The presence of God's kingdom follows with those who trust in God as King. The kingdom is shared first in a God-to-person relationship, and then in our person-to-person relationships. A chain reaction of copycats has taken place.

The most important thing that Jesus wanted to leave with us was that people like us have the power and the authority to advance the Kingdom of God! It's our choice. Internal adjustment leads to external action. Remember in Chapter 6 when Jesus made the transition of sharing his work with us? What did he tell the disciples to say to the people whom they had healed? *The Kingdom of God is near you now.*[14]

---

[13] Matt. 3:2, 4:17.

[14] Luke 10:9.

Open for All

Erikson's original insight about generativity vs. self-absorption raises a great question: Is God's kingdom established in our hearts? If it is, then clearly caring for the next generation will be revealed in the wake of everything we do. The selfless nature of Christ invades the crudely constructed battlements of our selfish hearts and sets up a domain that would provide a new direction not just for ourselves or even for our immediate families, but also for all who are to come. The rule of God's kingdom establishes new pathways as self-interest gives way to putting others first. Midlife crisis averted!

We do have plenty of things in common, don't we? We are all copycats of someone else, we all have been through one process or another of learning, and we each have the ability to change. Yet, even now, we may have counted ourselves out as being unable to trust God, let alone ourselves. Think about this: Just as we are prone to thinking only of ourselves thanks to our own inherited sinful nature, we can become alive when as God's adopted sons and daughters we inherit his Holy Spirit, and find we love our neighbors as ourselves. We all have the same opportunity to change our direction, a gift of *turning*, because the kingdom is near.

Shared

Kosta (Gus) Portokalos is a stubborn hulk of a man in one of my favorite movies, "*My Big Fat Greek Wedding*." Gus takes it upon himself to educate everyone he meets about which words have Greek roots. He shares at his daughter's wedding about their family name and likens it to his son-in-law's last name, Miller.

You know, the root of the word Miller is a Greek word. Miller come from the Greek word "milo," which is mean "apple," so there you go. As many of you know, our name, Portokalos, is come from the Greek word "portokali," which mean "orange." So, okay? Here tonight, we have, ah, apple and orange. We all different, but in the end, we are all fruit![15]

We are all fruit. Our common bond with God and with one another is to be shared. The kingdom actually grows as our church communities interact with God and with each other. Don't worry; we don't lose the positive elements of our cultural identities when we recognize our oneness in God. Certainly, we can't help but be changed into becoming more forgiving, more merciful, more caring. People the world over have an opportunity to experience God's kingdom. As God builds his church, we look forward to the hope that one day all would experience God's kingdom![16]

Without this perspective that the Gospel is meant for everyone, shared with the whole world, we might find ourselves hiding behind things, material stuff, that blocks our willingness to take his kingdom to the world. Generative vs. self-absorption.

When we decide to stop caring, that's when we begin to exclude people from our lives. We splinter and fall apart.

Then children were brought to him that he might lay his hands on them and pray. The disciples rebuked the people, but Jesus said, "Let the little children come to me and do not hinder them, for to

[15] *"My Big Fat Greek Wedding."* HBO Home Video, 2003.

[16] Isa. 2:2.

such belongs the kingdom of heaven." And he laid his hands on them and went away.[17]

Of all people to keep away from Jesus, the disciples kept out the kids. These are the same disciples who spent time arguing about which one of them would be the most important in the kingdom of God.[18] By saying "Follow Me" Jesus gave the disciples a command so simple that a child could understand. They had heard Jesus talk about the kingdom many times, but not like this. Jesus said the kingdom belonged to those whose faith is as simple and as trusting as a child's. This might make us want to reprimand the disciples for wanting to keep the children away from Jesus. Let's look at ourselves for a moment. Do we really want to help the next generation? The fact is they will copycat something or rather someone. So the only question is, who are they going to copycat? Will we volunteer to be a part of the process of changing the course of the world by being copycats and mentors who care for the *least of these*?

Rich and Young

The path toward a midlife crisis and a failed generational transfer of God's blessing starts well before age fifty. Our heart's direction can be set while we are still young children. When a young ruler who had power and wealth to spare rolled up to ask Jesus a question, the events as they unfolded left him feeling justified in himself.

---

[17] Matt. 19:13-15.

[18] Matt. 18:1; Luke 10:9.

Just then a man came up to Jesus and asked, "Teacher, what good thing must I do to get eternal life?"

"Why do you ask me about what is good?" Jesus replied. "There is only One who is good. If you want to enter life, keep the commandments."

"Which ones?" he inquired.

Jesus replied, "You shall not murder, you shall not commit adultery, you shall not steal, you shall not give false testimony, honor your father and mother,' and 'love your neighbor as yourself.'"

"All these I have kept," the young man said. "What do I still lack?"

Jesus answered, "If you want to be perfect, go, sell your possessions and give to the poor, and you will have treasure in heaven. Then come, follow me."

When the young man heard this, he went away sad, because he had great wealth.[19]

Even under all the layers of righteous talk and deeds, this young man had a heart problem. He was unwilling to trust God completely with his heart, and so he failed the test when Jesus challenged him to part with his possessions. Erickson would have said he was *self-absorbed.* How would we respond if Jesus asked us the same question? Although we may have loved our neighbor as ourselves, been good, and not hurt anyone, have we sought to put ourselves first instead of our children? Will we gain the world and lose our souls, or will we lose the world and gain the kingdom?

---

[19] Matt. 19:16-22.

One thing is for sure: Copycats will copy our decision.

Conclusion

God's kingdom on earth happens through a community guided by shepherds who care and are close by. How we have used our original gifting to create relationships between people and God will define our reputation. If we will leave the ninety-nine to rescue the one sheep that went astray, we will be known by our actions. If we stay with the ninety-nine and forget the one, we will be known by our actions.

All of us have the gift of copycatting others. The direction of our mimesis is incredibly important. Rather than cheating off another's exam paper, we instead give credit for original ideas, and we come closer to pioneering new pathways.

Study Questions:

1. What distinguishes a life that is generative from a life that is self-absorbed?
2. Internal adjustments lead to external action. What changes might you need to make in your heart so that Jesus would be seen and heard in your world?

Chapter 9

Atmosphere

No legacy is so rich as honesty. – William Shakespeare

If something happens, something else happens. When I drink all of my coffee, I will inevitably want more. If you combine Mexican cuisine with capitalism, factoring in human error, you then get Taco Bell. Take Math. If Suzie finds a basket full of apples and a basket holds twelve apples, then how many apples did Suzie find? In the Bible however, *"If my people, who are called by my name, will humble themselves and pray and seek my face and turn from their wicked ways, then I will hear from heaven, and I will forgive their sin and will heal their land."*[1]

If/then statements connect two separate events together in a sequential relationship. The *if* is a condition; when it is fulfilled, *then* something else will happen. *If/then* is found in every decision, thought, and movement. This simple way of explaining relationships creates atmospheres. Each atmosphere is an awareness and proximity of: attitude, intention, and the presence or the absence of love.

We, as humans, have the ability to create our own opinion. A bar of chocolate, if 70 percent cacao and above, will taste great

---

[1] 2 Chronicles 14.

(dare I say *delicious*) to some, will be snubbed by lovers of milk chocolate, or ignored altogether by chocolate agnostics. Some will salivate, some will shake their heads, and some will shrug their shoulders. We learn to judge whether something is good or bad from others. Pizza, burgers, salads, or fruit, can all become acceptable food when introduced a number of times with positive impressions.[2] Our tastes are acquired by copycatting our parents or others.

If you learned that something was good, then it is good; conversely, if something was bad, it is bad. Our learned preferences directly affect the *if/then* statements in our hearts and minds. If our doctor pokes us with too many needles, then we might run in the opposite direction when it comes time for our annual physical. Our moments of pain, flight, joy, and taste merge to create the atmosphere that we live in. When other people experience us, they experience our atmosphere.

The good news is that these ideas and fears can be overcome through professional help (especially for the chocolate-haters) and positive modeling. This harkens back to Chapter 4 and finding a mentor to follow. By copycatting a mentor, the process of discipleship will change our atmosphere. Even our opinions may begin to change for the better. Instead of ideas that disregard God, we might begin to experience ideas that include him. Through a positive, Christ-centered atmosphere, others will begin to realize they are loved,[3] they have become God's

---

[2] Department of Psychology, University of Roehampton, London, "A Narrative Review of Psychologoical and Educational Strategies," 85.

[3] John 3:16.

children.[4] They can live sacrificially,[5] and they can share God's caring nature with others.[6] The atmosphere of their hearts will be wholly changed![7] Those things that once were seen as dangerous and distasteful are now seen in a new light. Those relationships once despised can become a new way of life.

Regarding God, seven billion opinions grace our human race. What children believe about God is greatly influenced by their parents and home culture. One study found that if a social atmosphere has a detrimental effect on a child, it primarily has a "negative" effect on their belief system as well.[8] A culture of disbelief or rigid legalism will certainly affect the *if/then* statements that a child lives by. Their daily decisions, both good and bad, will impact not only their own future, but conceivably everyone they meet. More than ever before, mentors need to claim their place in the family and the church, creating an atmosphere of belief.

Weather

Few topics are so fascinating and unavoidable as the weather. Based on where we live in the world, we can spend anywhere from six to ten months of our lives talking about the weather![9] It's one of the most common ways to start a conversation because

---

[4] Rom. 8:14.

[5] Phil. 2: 5-7.

[6] Mark 12: 30-31.

[7] 2 Cor. 5:17.

[8] Blackwell, "Implicit Theories of Intelligence Predict Achievement Across an Adolescent Transition," 259-260.

[9] Adams, "Britons 'Spend Six Months Talking About Weather,'" para. 2.

it is an indirect variable that any two people can relate to—in other words, it's safe. Most people beginning language studies focus on landmarks, food, and weather.

It is the atmosphere we inhabit that really matters most in terms of determining how we live. In a revealing study about the effect of weather on conversation, psychologists found that people already in a bad mood use the weather to explain their feelings at that moment.[10] Those who were in a good mood usually paid the weather no mind at all.

Our own personal outlook directly affects how we perceive our surroundings. Furthermore, while our preferences make no difference as to how the weather behaves, the atmosphere of our attitude decides largely how we react to it. In other words, it could be a sunny, beautiful day, and yet a person with a negative atmosphere about them might well grumble about it anyway.

Some people will consistently look for things to blame and accuse, rather than finding opportunities to bless. The atmosphere that they were born into might have been one of *if/ then* statements of negativity.

By today's technology our best meteorologists can measure and predict the weather, but even our greatest innovations (apart from our contribution of pollution) cannot create weather systems. We were born into an atmosphere that was made to sustain us.

What atmosphere have we been gifted to create then? What does this suggest to us about the atmosphere that we create in our homes and faith communities?

---

[10] Schwarz and Clore, "Mood, Misattribution, and Judgments of Well-Being," 5.

The Ecosystem of the Church

Deeply rooted in our homes and churches is an atmosphere created by the hearts of its inhabitants. In these places of great influence, as someone copycats you, they in some way will be exposed to your convictions, opinions, *if/thens*, and beliefs. Your atmosphere affects your closest family, friends, and mentees. Considering that the church is a calling-out[11] of many to trust in Jesus Christ and his promises, each person carries an atmosphere with him or her. Since people are so indescribably different, it must be expected that opinions will collide and perspectives differ.

I ask then that the older ones among us step out first and begin pouring ourselves into the younger, that mentors would be available to mentees. All age groups have something to contribute. To those who are older, it is not just your resources that is asked of you. To those who are younger, it is not just your energy that's needed. Learning from present-day examples of Christ in our midst opens up the opportunity for each person in the church to copycat those behaviors regardless of age. This is the ecosystem of the church, where an atmosphere of discipleship and mentorship takes place.

The Difference

We all are copycats.

We see a behavior, and if it benefits us or helps us reach a goal, we try to emulate the person exhibiting that behavior; he or she becomes our mentor. The global church is made up of groups

---

[11] Thomas, *New American Standard Hebrew–Aramaic and Greek Dictionaries*, 1537, 2564.

of people from all walks of life. Anticipating that we would need a mentor who would unite us, God sent the Holy Spirit to change our hearts. Not confined to family bloodlines, the Spirit begins his work in the midst of hurt, pain, and doubt. Jesus sends us a great promise that's found in Matthew 18:20: "For where two or three gather in my name, there am I with them."

When hearts are turned toward God, given the example that Jesus is to us, there is no better place for us to start than to follow a shepherd so near to us that we share in the same Spirit. We have a mentor to copycat and a process to grow through.

To the believer, when this occurs, negativity subsides, and joy increases. To those not-yet-believing, the opportunity is present to place trust in Jesus Christ, someone they may have never considered. He was there even before the beginning of time and will still be there at the end of all things. Our true selves are found by becoming copycats of God himself, because of Jesus Christ, the savior of all.

Jesus makes all the difference. Jesus sets the tone and creates the atmosphere; no one and nothing else will ever take his place. Jesus resides in the joyful praises/shouts/whispers of people who dare to speak his powerful name. Jesus takes the place of the bottle, the smoke, the craving, and the needle that people turn to in hopes of filling their emptiness. Jesus takes the place of the self-serving seeking personal gain. Jesus takes the place of the shattered mirror of a fragmented self-image. Jesus takes the place of the open wounds of physical abuse. Jesus takes the place of the angry words in a cheerless marriage. Jesus takes the place of our tear-stained rags of self-pity.

The sum of the parts of the church is a group of copycats who know they are broken, but who continually subject themselves to change, together. There is an unspeakable joy that fills a heart that comes to live in an atmosphere devoted to Christ.

Jesus calls us to copycat, to follow him. He calls us to forgive, to care, to bind up the wounds, to relieve the pain, to send, to go, to live, to shout, to sit, to stand, to run, and to offer peace and hope to the lost.

Go and do likewise. Copycat.

Appendix
Be a Copycat – Express Yourself

If you have ever doubted, downplayed, or ignored your own creative spark, you should do yourself and your loved ones a solid favor by developing the originality that you already hold within you. There are plenty of professional artists who keep quiet about their creative process. I gain great joy in demystifying how those who wish to mentor others express themselves through this process. In this Appendix, I will briefly share my own simple creative process and also some tips that may help you. Hopefully these suggestions will guide you toward your own artistic work, whatever the medium might be. By all good reason, use your gift to copycat and unleash your creativity!

Here, I would like to focus on your artistic idea, and the process we can use to develop it. Words, notes, and shapes do not pop into our heads simply because of our will to make it happen. For those inspired to begin, yet are avoiding doing so out of timidity or for some silly reason like fear—let's try to create something today. Let's make the effort.

My Process

Our challenge is to harness your inspirational spark. Together, through a creative process let's form something, shaping it to come as close to the embodiment of your original inspiration as possible. I'll take you through my own creative process in writing this book, following the four steps that were illustrated in Chapter 3: Desire, Decide, Design, and Do.

Copycatting is a highly effective way to learn something new, right?

Desire

My desire to create didn't start with needing to write a book. It began with a question that intrigued me, that kept me thinking late at night, with more thoughts greeting me as I woke the next day. After awhile, I couldn't keep everything organized in my head, and needed to write down my ponderings in order to develop the idea.

What is your idea? What keeps your mind wondering? Further, what form of art are you interested in?

It is important to not envision the finished work of art. Try to think only about the action of trying. Consider a wheel that spins and spins. Think of a waterfall where the water cascades in a seemingly unending deluge. Working at your craft with these images in mind fosters a perpetual loop of practice. We try, try, and try again. Have you ever heard someone trying to learn how to play the violin? What horrendous noise! Yet if they keep at it, the sound changes from screeching cats to a much more emotive tone. Working with an art form develops precision and accuracy, making it easier and easier to get our inner creative impulses out into the open. Whatever the finished product of art that you treasure, be it film, music, sculpture, painting, you are seeing the result of thousands of hours of practice. Blood, sweat, and tears. The *desire* to create pushes you to create through almost any obstacle.

As my desire to create overwhelmed me, the words needed to come out onto paper! I couldn't bottle them up any longer. I needed to do something about the question I was carrying around with me. When we let our desire to create grow, we are left with a solidified *idea* that is waiting for our *decision* to do something about it.

I'm of the mind that ideas, truly great ideas, are born of process. *Process* tests, pulls, squishes, and stretches the idea to its limits. Jot down pros and cons to see if the original thought you had will survive.

Follow other artists: Copycat them

Chances are, reading other authors, listening to albums, visiting the theater or art galleries, is what inspired you in the first place, where you first realized the power of self-expression. The best teachers are those who wish for their students to do *greater things* than they did. Follow the process that other artists are utilizing. Look at the healthy habits they develop. The rules they follow in creating their art can tell you much of what to do and what not to do. So it was with Jesus. He obeyed certain practices that God had set forth for him to follow; and as he lived according to those guidelines, a new way of life for all the world was born!

Copycat other artists and the good habits they developed in their creative process. We must capture the inspirational spark that is *desire* with a *decision* to do something with it.

Decide

Many have endeavored to do something artistic. Not having a finished product to show for their efforts, they considered themselves beaten down by writer's block, stage fright, cramped fingers, laryngitis, an unfinished album—and they abandoned their inspired beginning. There are thousands, if not millions, of unfinished pieces of art in this world. This is a small tragedy.

We must *decide* to do something about our *desire*. If we do not purposefully add effort to our creative thoughts, we will have to live with undocumented and unfulfilled intention.

We could all use some more *attempted* intentions, right? Regardless of whether we reach our goal, a hope, a creative spark preceded our attempts. Be warned: doubt, timidity, and fear will do everything they can to stop us from acting on these inspired ideas. Once you decide to put your idea to work, don't look back!

Yoda, you see, was halfway correct. (I do mean the Yoda from *"Star Wars" and not* Yoda, my dog.) "Do or do not. There is no try." He was right and wrong at the same time.

There's always room to try. Our individual vision and innovation develop when we begin to discover ways to communicate them externally. Artistic expression is meant to evoke action and emotion. Those actions and emotions may never happen if you do not try to put forth any effort at all.

Make a *decision* to make the effort because of the *desire* overwhelming your heart and mind. Once this threshold has been crossed, we will need to create a *design* for our inspired idea.

Design

I knew that just thinking about the question wouldn't be good enough for me. I needed to give shape to the idea. I found myself on a flight to Dallas when I realized my mind couldn't contain my idea any longer. I opened up a piece of outlining software on my computer and let the ideas pour onto the screen. I didn't restrain myself, either. Soon I had two pages of undeveloped text. I let the ideas continue to flow. After that,

wherever I went, I kept with me a small notebook. Whether at
the coffee shop, home, or work, I would jot down my thoughts. I
treated my thoughts as worthy to be written down.

This is an important step. Take your steps toward artistic
expression seriously.

I would later transfer my ideas from my notebook to my
developing outline. My idea was growing, and as I followed
where it led, I learned more and more. I got curious and
researched my idea. Both the outline and the portable notebook
were integral to me setting a *design* to my creativity.

I must have started five hundred sentences that went
absolutely nowhere in writing this book. My misguided thoughts
or poorly researched ideas fell flat by the time I was searching for
the correct punctuation to finish each phrase. That's part of the
design. Some ideas can be unfocused, written down, and then
deleted … and that's okay! Some songs, paintings, and scripts are
simply … bad. No condemnation, no fear, only creativity. One
can always separate the wheat from the chaff at a later time.

The *design* of a song, written work, or painting provides a
frame on which to flesh out the original idea. For our creativity
to be understood, it must be given a *design*, a structured
environment within which we can *do* the work of art.

Do

Once the outline and characteristics of what you want to
develop are noted for your own reference, it is then time to
create. The discipline of whatever medium you have repeatedly
practiced is now going to help your desire to form and shape
them.

We receive a certain responsibility when we receive inspiration, namely, to take it through a time of testing. Our *attempted intention*, at this stage of the creative process, can become a *proven idea.*

Start

The walk of a thousand miles starts not with a step, but with someone first getting up off the couch. In our pursuit of producing something, there can be a million thoughts that run through our heads. "What guitar will I use?"—"What kind of paint is best?"—"I need a new computer!"

Whatever that *thing* is which you deem to be absolutely necessary to begin creating, can actually become an obstacle to getting your original idea effectively out into real life.

Sit down and put pen to paper, strum that chord, stand at the edge of the empty auditorium and recite some lines from your script. Work with what you already have! Believe in what you are about to create. Look back on the work you performed. Ask yourself: Did my idea come one step closer to reality? If not, then rework it. Your original idea must build interest and understanding as you invite others to relate to your art.

Pour thought and creativity into your art as much as you are able to. It can be tempting to say to yourself that you are going to write every day. Don't. It may be a promise that you cannot keep, and if you try and fail, you will only wind up wearing yourself down! Break the habit of cookie cutter creations! Some of the greatest twists and *gotcha* moments in songs and writing come from ideas that were ordered differently.

You can do this.

Here are some things to consider that can greatly assist you in the *Do* step of the creative process.

Set Creative Rules

Your rules will not only guide you when the artistic idea is hard to describe, but they might just save you from total disaster.

Your creativity deserves boundaries or *rules*. Honestly, I am excited! Usually we like to buck trends, yet as you have read through *Copycat*, hopefully you have discovered that we all have the ability to pioneer our own creative works.

This is one of the most helpful suggestions that has guided my own work. Before I fleshed out the essence of my idea, I developed a Rules Sheet. You might like to do your own thing, but I found that in order to learn, it helps to copycat someone else and their approach to creating.

Here's my list of rules (for writing)!

My rules for writing at my best are these:

- I'm going to try and keep punctuation to a minimum, as you have an imagination and therefore can imagine the timbre and inflection in words and phrases.
- I'm going to write shorter sentences instead of trying to pack too much into one sentence that doesn't know when to stop.
- I'm conservative in my theology.
- I'm sticking to the outline.
- Write about what I'm going to communicate.
- Keep it interesting.
- Stop writing when it ceases to be interesting.

- Don't write about anything that is mere speculation. Leave that to others who are more knowledgeable.
- Don't write as though you're an expert, but as a person who doesn't know enough about the subject to become a fanatic. My hopes for you are not fanatical, but practical.
- Be yourself. I will never be cool enough for some people. Sadly we will never hang out together, and they will never find out how correct they really are.
- Use your own ideas and ask permission of others when you use their ideas to illustrate your point. Acknowledge their ideas.

Rules keep you on course, and keep you true to your goal. Develop this sheet early on in your writing. It will save your creativity from dead ends.

Setting

Setting makes a difference. Consider a soldier in combat writing a letter to his loved ones from the front-line trenches while shells explode and bullets fly. Does the setting in which he writes determine his tone? Might he not write about things that matter while his life is at risk?

Our conditions and environment have the ability to determine the intensity, tone, and even the message that we might choose to communicate. To get that proven idea out into an artistic form, deliberately choosing a setting is foundational to true expression. One of the great benefits of tailoring your own workspace is that you can then limit the influences and distractions that might detract from your art.

Many graphic designers and photographers working in true-color paint their surrounding workspaces in a medium gray. This background acts as a canvas for vision, assisting artists and viewers to see the created works in their full array without any distraction from unrelated sources. Authors, musicians, painters, sculptors should keep in mind the neutrality of their setting so that the passion communicated through the creative process can inspire the full spectrum of their imagination. Whatever setting you have available to you, don't be afraid of keeping it uncluttered, boring, and predictable. The contrast between your setting and the art at hand can then be clearly delineated, keeping you focused on the task at hand. You are at your workspace to create with intent.

Whether sitting in a secluded room or in the middle of an open field makes no difference. Find a place where you can *turn off the rest of the world* while you create.

Lock the door if possible. Background music is up to you. Forget about TV. Forget about your cell phone; put it on silent or turn it off. People look at their phones on average one hundred fifty times a day. Somehow the world will continue to spin without your contribution to global social media.

What you are looking for is a zone of flow. It may sound odd, but once your words, notes, music, and thoughts start to flow, you'll thank yourself that you limited your distractions.

After you have a developed idea as a result of *desire, decide, design, do,* I have an unlikely plan for your work.

Resurrection

It may sound overtly Christian, yet this principle stands true. If an idea is worth expressing and expounding on, try forgetting about it. Take your finished work, and if possible, place it into a file cabinet, put it into a corner of the basement, store it in the attic. Try to forget about it. If your idea is really worth exploring, it will return to you in time with more life in it than when you first left it!

For me, my trusted neighbor Michael provided the test and the signal that my original idea for *Copycat*, three years later, would be resurrected. Over coffee in the afternoon, I pitched my outline for the idea. I let him stress-test it with questions, ponder the idea, and tell me his own thoughts. I let him share his thoughts both positive and negative about my idea because he was a trusted person. In the end, he encouraged me to write about it. The idea had new life!

If the idea is fragile and weak, that will be revealed during this waiting time, only to crumble as you revisit it. If it is a good idea, a true thought, it will be resurrected.

These are the things that I hope for in your pursuit, that you would feel a deep sense of responsibility in carrying your idea (to a Frodo-esque level) and that you would allow the idea to die and to be resurrected. I hope your art would find new life and you would find a renewed inspiration through it all.

With a resurrected idea and because of this creative process you can step into your workspace with confidence that (1) you have a great idea worth exploring and investing time in, and (2) that the idea is crafted in such a way that it's received by others ready to hear what you have to say.

God bless your pursuit of your originality!

Bibliography

Adams, Stephen. *"Britons 'Spend Six months Talking About Weather."'* *Telegraph,* May 7, 2010. http://www.telegraph.co.uk/news/weather/7718963/Britons-spend-six-months-talking-about-weather.html.

Aurelius, Marcus, Thomas Gataker, André Dacier, Jeremy Collier, and Marcus Cebes. *Emperor Marcus Antoninus: His Conversation With Himself.* London: Richard Sare, 1701.

Bandura, Albert. "Social Cognitive Theory: An Agentic Perspective." *Annual Review of Psychology* 52 (2001): 1-26.

Bevans, Stephen B. *Models of Contextual Theology.* Maryknoll: Orbis, 2011.

Blackwell, Lisa S., Kali H. Trzesniewski, and Carol Sorich Dweck. "Implicit Theories of Intelligence Predict Achievement Across an Adolescent Transition: A Longitudinal Study and an Intervention." *Child Development* 78:1 (Jan/Feb 2007): 260.

Bosch, David J. *Transforming Mission: Paradigm Shifts in Theology of Mission.* Maryknoll: Orbis, 1991.

British Library. "Gutenberg Bible: The Basics." http://www.bl.uk/treasures/gutenberg/basics.html.

Brown, Jim. "Shepherd." Compiled by Phil Zarns. Brussels, February 20, 2012.

Cabal, Ted, ed. *The Apologetics Study Bible: Real Questions, Straight Answers, Stronger Faith.* Nashville: Holman, 2007.

Campbell, Iain D. *Opening Up Exodus.* Leominster: Day One, 2006.

Centers for Disease Control and Prevention. *"Learn the Signs, Act Early: Milestones 4 months."* *National Center on Birth Defects and Developmental Disabilities.* Compiled by Steven Shelov. July 5, 2012. http://www.cdc.gov/ncbddd/actearly/milestones/milestones-4mo.html.

Cnn Tees. *"Coke vs. Pepsi: The History of the Cola Wars."* 2011. http://www.cnntees.com/infographics/coke-vs-pepsi-the-cola-wars.

Collins, Gary R. *Christian Counseling: A Comprehensive Guide.* Nashville: Thomas Nelson, 1988.

Collins, Jim. *Good to Great: Why Some Companies Make the Leap... And Others Don't.* New York: HarperCollins, 2001.

Collins, Keith. *Academy Awards.* March 2014. http://hosted.ap.org/interactives/2014/oscars.

Colton, Rev. Caleb Charles. *Lacon: Or, Many Things In Few Words.* London: Longman, Orme, Brown, Greene & Longmans, 1837.

Danielson, Oriel. *"The Perfect Soda."* Documentary. Directed by Oriel Danielson. Performed by Oriel Danielson. 2013.

Department of Psychology, University of Roehampton, London. "A Narrative Review of Psychological and Educational Strategies Applied to Young Children's Eating Behaviours Aimed at Reducing Obesity Risk." *Obesity Reviews* 1 (March 2012): 85-95.

Dickens, Leah, and David DeSteno. "Pride Attenuates Nonconscious Mimicry." *Emotion* 14:1 (2014): 7-11.

Dockery, David S., ed. *Holman Bible Handbook.* Nashville: Holman, 1992.

Draper, Charles W., Chad Brand, and Archie England, eds. *Holman Illustrated Bible Dictionary.* Nashville: Holman, 2003.

Dyer, Frank Lewis, and Thomas Commerford Martin. *Edison: His Life and Inventions.* Amazon, 2012. Kindle edition.

Dylan, Bob. "You Gotta Serve Somebody." *Slow Train Coming.* 1979.

Eims, Leroy. *The Lost Art of Disciple Making.* Grand Rapids: Zondervan, 1978.

Einstein, Albert. "Letter from Albert Einstein to President Franklin Delano Roosevelt." Long Island: National Archives, 1939.

Ellsworth, Roger. *Opening Up Psalms.* Leominster: Day One Publications, 2006.

Erikson, Erik H., and Joan M. Erikson. *The Life Cycle Completed (Extended Version).* New York: W. W. Norton & Company, 1998. Kindle edition.

Falkenstein, Eric. "A Batesian Mimicry Explanation of Business
  Cycles." July 26, 2010. http://falkenblog.blogspot.se/
  2010/07/batesian-mimicry-explanation-of.html.
Firstenberg, Ofer, Thibault Peyronel, Qi-Yu Liang, Alexey V.
  Gorshkov, Mikhail D. Lukin, and Vladan Vuletic.
  "Attractive Photons in a Quantum Nonlinear Medium."
  Nature 502 (October 3, 2013): 71-75.
Freeman, James M. *The New Manners and Customs of the Bible.*
  Updated by Harold J. Chadwick. North Brunswick: Bridge,
  1998.
Fullerton, George. *Guitars from George and Leo: How Leo Fender
  and I Built G&L Guitars.* Victoria: Hal Leonard, 2005.
Gamberale-Stille, G., A., C. V. Balogh, B. S. Tullberg, and O.
  Leimar. "Feature Saltation and the Evolution of Mimicry."
  Evolution 66:3 (March 2012): 807-817.
Gladwell, Malcolm. *The Tipping Point: How Little Things Can
  Make a Big Difference.* New York: Back Bay, 2002.
Gray, Richard. "Sheep Are Far Smarter Than Previously
  Thought." *Telegraph,* February 20, 2011. http://
  www.telegraph.co.uk/science/science-news/8335465/Sheep-
  are-far-smarter-than-previously-thought.html.
Greene, Andy. "Readers' Poll: The 10 Worst Bob Dylan Songs."
  Rolling Stone. http://www.rollingstone.com/music/pictures/
  readers-poll-the-10-worst-bob-dylan-songs-20130703/2-
  gotta-serve-somebody-0393106.
Harmon, Dion, Marcus A. M. de Aguiar, David D. Chinellato,
  Dan Braha, Irving R. Epstein, and Yaneer Bar-Yam.
  "Predicting Economic Market Crises Using Measures of
  Collective Panic." Study by the New England Complex
  Systems Institute, Universidade Estadual de Campinas,
  Dartmouth, Cambridge, 2011.
Harrison, Burton. *Bar Harbor Days.* New York: Harper &
  Brothers, 1887.
Jaktlund, Carl-Henrik. "Den Stora Kyrkflykten" ["The Big Move
  of the Church"]. *Dagen,* January 29, 2009. http://
  www.dagen.se/vardag/den-stora-kyrkflykten-del-2.

KidsHealth.org. *"Plagiarism."* Edited by Stephen Dowshen. September 1, 1994. http://kidshealth.org/kid/feeling/school/plagiarism.html#.

King, Stephen. *On Writing: A Memoir of The Craft*. New York: Pocket, 2000.

Kinnaman, Doug. "Six Reasons Young Christians Leave Church." *Barna*, September 28, 2011. http://www.barna.org/teens-next-gen-articles/528-six-reasons-young-christians-leave-church.

Knowles, Andrew. *The Bible Guide. 1st ed*. Minneapolis: Augsburg, 2001.

Koeshall, John and Anita. "Redeemed Power in Action: A Prerequisite for a Generous Ecclesiology." Paper presented at Assemblies of God Theological Seminary, Springfield, MO. November 2011.

Ladd, George Eldon. *A Theology of the New Testament*. Edited by Donald A. Hagner. Grand Rapids: Wm. B. Eerdmans Publishing Company, 1993.

Lally, P., C. H. M. van Jaarsveld, H. W. W. Potts, and J. Wardle. "How Are Habits Formed: Modelling Habit Formation in the Real World." *European Journal of Social Psychology* 40:6 (July 2009): 998-1009.

Lee, Stan. *Stan's Soapbox: The Collection*. The Hero Initiative, 2008.

Life Application Bible: New International Version. Grand Rapids, MI: Zondervan, 1991.

Longman, Tremper, and Raymond B. Dillard. *An Introduction to the Old Testament*. Grand Rapids: Zondervan, 1994.

Marshall, I. Howard, A. R. Millard, J. I. Packer, and D. J. Wiseman, eds. *New Bible Dictionary. 3rd ed*. Downers Grove: InterVarsity, 1996.

Maslow, Abraham. "A Theory of Human Motivation." *Psychological Review* 50:4 (1943).

McMillian, John. *Beatles vs. Stones*. New York: Simon & Schuster, 2013.

Merriam-Webster Dictionary. Merriam-Webster, 2005.

Mona Lisa Foundation. "Summary of Scientific and Physical Examinations." *Mona Lisa*, March 20, 2013. http://

monalisa.org/2013/03/20/summary-of-scientific-physical-examinations.

Mörling, Nicklas. Interview by Phil Zarns. March 2013.

Morris, Leon. *The Epistle to the Romans.* Grand Rapids: Wm. B. Eerdmans, 1988.

Murray, Andrew. *Humility and Absolute Surrender.* Peabody: Hendrickson, 2005.

Nanos, Mark D. *The Mystery of Romans: The Jewish Context of Paul's Letter.* Minneapolis: Fortress, 1996.

Newton, Sir Isaac. *The Mathematical Principles of Natural Philosophy.* Amazon, 2013.

Nobel Prize in Physics 1906. http://www.nobelprize.org/nobel_prizes/physics/laureates/1906.

Nobel Prize. "Otto Hahn - Facts." http://www.nobelprize.org/nobel_prizes/chemistry/laureates/1944/hahn-facts.html.

O'Connell, Kate. "Happy Birthday, Copy Machine! Happy Birthday, Copy Machine!" *NPR,* October 23, 2013. http://www.npr.org/2013/10/23/239241106/happy-birthday-copy-machine-happy-birthday-copy-machine.

Office for Research Integrity. "Plagiarism of Ideas." http://ori.hhs.gov/plagiarism-4.

Olson, K. R., and A. Shaw. "No Fair, Copycat! What Children's Response to Plagiarism Tells Us About Their Understanding of Ideas." *Developmental Science* 14:2 (September 2010): 431-439.

Owen, David. *Copies in Seconds: How a Lone Inventor and an Unknown Company Created the Biggest Communication Breakthrough Since Gutenberg.* New York: Simon & Schuster, 2008.

PBS. "Babies Are Natural Copycats." *PBS.* http://www.pbs.org/parents/child-development/baby-and-toddler/babies-are-natural-copycats.

Prime, Derek. *Opening Up 1 Corinthians.* Leominister: Day One, 2005.

Qualls, Joy. "Theology Belongs to the Artists as Much As It Does the Apologists." Lecture given at the National Communication Association 99th Annual Convention, Washington, D.C., November 21, 2013.

Rankine, William. *On the General Law of the Transformation of Energy*. Glasgow, 1853.

Rawls, Wilson. *Where the Red Fern Grows*. New York: Yearling, 1996.

Richards, Lawrence O. *The Bible Reader's Companion: Your Guide to Every Chapter of the Bible*. Wheaton: Victor, 1991. Kindle edition.

Ritland, David B., and Lincoln P. Brower. "The Viceroy Butterfly Is Not a Batesian Mimic." *Nature* 350 (April 1991): 497-498.

Rock and Roll Hall of Fame. "Leo Fender Biography." http://rockhall.com/inductees/leo-fender/bio.

Rorimer, James J. "The Mona Lisa." The Metropolitan Museum of Art Bulletin, February 1963: 223-224.

Schwarz, Norbert, and Gerald L. Clore. "Mood, Misattribution, and Judgments of Well-Being: Informative and Directive Functions of Affective States." *Journal of Personality and Social Psychology* 45:3 (September 1983): 513-523.

Sigfrids, Stefan. "DBS." *Stockholm*, January 9, 2014.

Stanley, Charles. *How to Listen to God*. Nashville: Thomas Nelson, 2002.

Stel, M., and R. Vonk. "Mimicry in Social Interaction: Benefits for Mimickers, Mimickees, and Their Interaction." *British Journal of Psychology* 101:2 (December 2010): 311-323.

Stevens, Bethan. "Spekphrasis: Writing About Lost Artworks; or, Mona Lisa and the Museum." *Critical Quarterly* 55:4 (December 2013): 54-64.

Strassner, Kurt. *Opening Up Genesis*. Leominster: Day One, 2009.

Stronstad, Roger. *Full Life Bible Commentary to the New Testament: An International Commentary for Spirit-Filled Christians*. Edited by French L. Arrington. Grand Rapids: Zondervan, 1999.

Subramanian, Courtney. "272,297 Dominoes Fall for New World Record." *Time,* July 18, 2013. http://newsfeed.time.com/2013/07/18/watch-272297-dominoes-fall-for-new-world-record.

Thomas, Robert L. *New American Standard Hebrew-Aramaic and Greek Dictionaries.* Nashville: Holman, 1981.

―――――. *New American Standard Hebrew-Aramaic and Greek Dictionaries: Updated Edition.* Anaheim: Foundation, 1998.

Thompson, Joseph J. "Carriers of Negative Electricity." December 11, 1906.

Utley, Robert James. *Luke the Historian: The Book of Acts. Vol. 3.* Marshall: Bible Lessons International, 2003.

Van Horen, Femke, and Rik Pieters. "When High-Similarity Copycats Lose and Moderate-Similarity Copycats Gain: The Impact of Comparative Evaluation." *Journal of Marketing Research* 49:1 (February 2012): 83-91.

Vejlgaard, Henrik. *Anatomy of a Trend.* New York: McGraw-Hill, 2012. Kindle edition.

Walvoord, John, and Roy Zuck, eds. *Bible Knowledge Commentary: An Exposition of the Scriptures by Dallas Seminary Faculty.* Wheaton, IL: Victor, 1985.

Wegren, Tom. "Songwriting." *Beethoven to Beatles.* December, 1995.

White, Forrest. *Fender: The Inside Story.* San Franciso: Backbeat, 1994.

Willard, Dallas. *The Divine Conspiracy: Rediscovering Our Hidden Life in God.* San Francisco: Harper Collins, 1997.

Wright, N. T. *Simply Christian: Why Christianity Makes Sense.* New York: HarperCollins, 2009. Kindle edition.

Zarns, Phil. *The Soundtrack of Your Life.* Phil Zarns, 2011. Kindle edition.

Zarns, Phil. "Transition Between Teenagers and Young Adults Within the Pentecostal Church of Sweden." Masters thesis, Assemblies of God Theological Seminary, 2012.

.

About the Author

Phil Zarns is interested in many things, among them God, family, a strong cup of black coffee, and guitar. More often than not, if there is an interesting story to be heard, he will be listening and trying to pick apart fact from fiction. He tries to use punctuation sparingly and often fails.

Husband to Katja and father to three inquisitive kids, Phil balances living between Sweden and the US, developing university ministry and church planting.

He grew up Lutheran and is an ordained pastor with the Assemblies of God.

Most important of all to Phil, he is a follower of Jesus Christ.

About ULP

Urban Loft Publishers focuses on ideas, topics, themes, and conversations about all things urban. Renewing the city is the central theme and focus of what we publish. It is our intention to blend urban ministry, theology, urban planning, architecture, urbanism, stories, and the social sciences as ways to drive the conversation. While we lean toward scholarly and academic works, we explore the fun and lighter sides of cities as well. We publish a wide variety of urban perspectives, from books by the experts about the city to personal stories and personal accounts of urbanites who live in the city.

urbanloftpublishers.com
@the_urban_loft

Made in the USA
Middletown, DE
18 September 2016